Praise for *Then They Came for Mine*

"If faith is something powerful—finding ways to tether human reality and divine love together—then that faith must be honest about the world but also reach toward healing. In *Then They Came for Mine*, Tracey Michae'l Lewis-Giggetts has not just offered a magnificent, searing, and soul-shaking narrative but has also found a way to do what the best sages, priests, and griots do: she has presented the world with revelation, the breath of the Spirit woven into the very fabric of Black life, literature, survival, art, artifacts, movement, possibility, and humanity. Part memoir, part mediation, part manifesto, this work has the character and skill of poetry, the brilliance of grace, the mystery of Black wisdom, and the illumination that the world we have been given is not all that there is to life. This book is affirmation. It is witness. It is lush. It is liberation. It is fire. It is spirit. It is testimony. It is gospel."

—**Danté Stewart**, author of *Shoutin' in the Fire: An American Epistle*

"Tracey Lewis-Giggetts is a master at weaving autobiographical narrative with cultural commentary, sharing her life experience and wisdom in such a way that it makes readers long to connect more deeply with their own. In *Then They Came for Mine*, she invites us to gaze at the wounds of racial trauma not as a sadomasochistic exercise but as a way to illuminate the way to hope and healing. This is not a book to be approached lightly. This is holy ground."

—**Chanequa Walker-Barnes**, Professor of Practical Theology and Pastoral Counseling, Columbia Theological Seminary

"So many of us are traumatized by the unbearably persistent and violent racism that is deeply woven into the fabric of our nation. Lewis-Giggetts knows the pain of loved ones murdered in racist attacks and also the pain of wounds that bleed invisibly, assailing our bodies and souls even as we carry on with the endurance of our ancestors. With passion and compassion, Lewis-Giggetts preaches that celebrations of so-called resilience and rushing to premature reconciliation will not heal our hearts, communities, or nation. Only by honestly exposing our wounds and speaking truth with fierce empathy and accountability can we heal the trauma that white supremacy has wrought on God's children of every ethnicity."

—**Jacqui Lewis,** author of *Fierce Love: A Bold Path to Ferocious Courage and Rule-Breaking Kindness That Can Heal the World* and *Ten Essential Strategies for Becoming a Multiracial Congregation*

"Anyone who desires whole mind-body-spirit healing from racial trauma should read this book. Timely, holistic, and insightful, Lewis-Giggetts's *Then They Came for Mine* is a trustworthy guide that I'll keep returning to in my personal healing journey and cite often in my professional work."

—**Christena Cleveland,** author of *God Is a Black Woman* and founder of the Center for Justice + Renewal

"Lewis-Giggetts offers a once-in-a-generation work with *Then They Came for Mine.* She weaves the personal testimonies of those whose loved ones have been killed by white supremacy and the histories of racial violence that undergird those events. Simply surviving the violence and rising to excellence fall short of our desires for a better future. In fact, 'resilience is making us sick,' writes Lewis-Giggetts, who calls the reader to choose 'healing over reconciliation.' Lewis-Giggetts provides a necessary challenge for anti-racist and trauma-informed healers, teachers, and leaders: center healing and love, for our lives and future generations depend on it."

—**Patrick B. Reyes**, author of *The Purpose Gap: Empowering Communities of Color to Find Meaning and Thrive*

"*Then They Came for Mine* provides an accessible and frank mind-body-spirit analysis of the kind of Christian faith needed to authentically respond to Black people's trauma caused by white racial violence. It is a timely resource for engaged faith community conversations about this violence."

—**Traci C. West**, author of *Solidarity and Defiant Spirituality: Africana Lessons on Religion, Racism, and Ending Gender Violence*

"With heart-wrenching narrative, astute analysis of Scripture, and unblinking passion, Lewis-Giggetts offers us a front-row seat to the very real impacts of systemic racism and what happens when it gets personal—and it's *always* personal. This is exactly the type of book that white people who claim to care about racial justice need to read, because it takes us from the comfortable upper echelons of the racialized body politic into the experience of a family living with the results of senseless racial violence. This story will forever change you. If you let it, it will change you for the better."

—**Kerry Connelly**, author of *Wait—Is This Racist?* and *Good White Racist?*

"By sharing very personal experiences, Tracey Lewis-Giggetts draws us in to recognize and affirm the blatant and nuanced manifestations of racism and the resultant racial trauma. Having experienced intense racial trauma at a very young age, I very much appreciate her intimate examination of what it's like to be Black in America. In refreshing conversational language, Lewis-Giggetts offers theological, sociological, historical, and legal perspectives on the complexities of racism and misogyny while examining the components lending them columnar support. Best of all, her very frank conversations about trauma are not offered to the exclusion of words about the human potential for faith, hope, and love."

—**Kevin Cosby**, President of Simmons College of
Kentucky and author of *Getting to the Promised Land*

THEN THEY CAME FOR MINE

Healing from the Trauma of Racial Violence

TRACEY MICHAE'L LEWIS-GIGGETTS

WESTMINSTER
JOHN KNOX PRESS
LOUISVILLE · KENTUCKY

First edition
Published by Westminster John Knox Press
Louisville, Kentucky

22 23 24 25 26 27 28 29 30 31—10 9 8 7 6 5 4 3 2 1

Unless otherwise indicated, Scripture quotations are from the New Revised Standard Version of the Bible, copyright © 1989 by the Division of Christian Education of the National Council of the Churches of Christ in the U.S.A., and are used by permission. Scripture quotations marked NIV are from *The Holy Bible, New International Version.* Copyright © 1973, 1978, 1984, 2011 by Biblica, Inc.® Used by permission. All rights reserved worldwide. Scripture quotations marked NLT are taken from the *Holy Bible,* New Living Translation, copyright 1996, 2004, 2015 by Tyndale House Foundation. Used by permission of Tyndale House Publishers, Inc., Carol Stream, Illinois 60188. All rights reserved. Scripture quotations marked TLB are taken from *The Living Bible* © 1971 by Tyndale House Foundation. Used by permission of Tyndale House Publishers, Inc., Carol Stream, Illinois 60188. All rights reserved.

Book design by Drew Stevens
Cover design by Mary Ann Smith
Cover art by Jawaan Burge. Used by permission.

Library of Congress Cataloging-in-Publication Data

Names: Lewis-Giggetts, Tracey M., author.
Title: Then they came for mine : healing from the trauma of racial violence
   / Tracey Michae'l Lewis-Giggetts.
Description: First edition. | Louisville, Kentucky : Westminster John Knox
   Press, [2022]
Identifiers: LCCN 2022017040 (print) | LCCN 2022017041 (ebook) | ISBN
   9780664267285 (paperback) | ISBN 9781646982707 (ebook)
Subjects: LCSH: Resilience (Personality trait) | Psychic trauma. | Race
   discrimination--Psychological aspects. | Black people--Psychology.
Classification: LCC BF698.35.R47 L49 2022 (print) | LCC BF698.35.R47
   (ebook) | DDC 155.2/408996--dc23/eng/20220302
LC record available at https://lccn.loc.gov/2022017040
LC ebook record available at https://lccn.loc.gov/2022017041

Most Westminster John Knox Press books are available at special quantity discounts when purchased in bulk by corporations, organizations, and special-interest groups. For more information, please e-mail SpecialSales@wjkbooks.com.

To Vickie
*I vowed that when you were taken from us, your death
would not only not be in vain but be a catalyst for repair
and restoration. My prayer is that this book honors you
and the glorious legacy of love and care you left behind.*

The basic fact is that Christianity as it was born in the mind of this Jewish thinker and teacher appears as a technique of survival for the oppressed. That it became, through the intervening years, a religion of the powerful and the dominant, used sometimes as an instrument of oppression, must not tempt us into believing that it was thus in the mind and life of Jesus. "In him was life; and the life was the light of men." Wherever his spirit appears, the oppressed gather fresh courage; for he announced the good news that fear, hypocrisy, and hatred, the three hounds of hell that track the trail of the disinherited, need have no dominion over them.

Howard Thurman,
Jesus and the Disinherited

CONTENTS

ACKNOWLEDGMENTS

It's always been incredibly important to me to hold the truth sacred. This, for me, has often meant living in the tension of my own lived experiences and the sometimes chaotic and heart-wrenching reality of this world of ours. And yet, there is truth in it all, isn't there? There is truth in every story. In every lineage. Good truth. Ugly truth. Sad truth. Joy-filled truth.

I think that's my intention here with this book. To unveil the truth of what it means to live as a Black person who feels forced to remain vigilant against violence and marginalization. To reveal the truth of how healing in the body, mind, and soul can begin for both survivor and oppressor. I hope I've done that work justice.

First and foremost, thank you to my cousins Mark and Sean, and my sorority sister Kellie, for lending your hearts and voices to this book. To Ena, who also shares their pain. To my White/Lewis family and the Stallard family: I was determined to honor this albatross of grief that we cannot shake and to make sure that the stealing of our precious family members' lives would not be in vain. My hope and prayer has always been that the names of Vickie Lee Jones and Maurice Stallard would live on and that transformation and healing would be the unexpected outcome from our tragedy.

Thank you so much to my parents for enduring my seemingly never-ending, public vulnerability and transparency. I know it's challenging for you, but I also know that you trust both my love for our family and my intent to live on purpose.

Thank you to my husband and sweet baby girl for loving me unconditionally and giving me the room and space to tell my stories. I hope to return that freedom to you in any way I can. You both breathe life into me daily.

Thank you to my agent, Cait Hoyt-Walden, at Creative Artists Agency for believing in me as a writer and a person. You listen to all my out-of-the-box and unwieldy ideas as I pull twenty years of projects out of the "vault."

Thank you so much to my amazing editor, Jessica Miller Kelley. It's been nine years since we first tried to work together, and I'm so grateful that, even now, you see the necessity of my work and the callings on my life.

Thank you to the entire team at Westminster John Knox Press for seeing the vision of this book and running with it. It's an enormous privilege to have a publishing team from my hometown working on such a deeply personal—and hopefully impactful—project.

Thank you, Holy Spirit, for that tug in my gut, for that awareness in my mind, for that discerning pull in my heart. I trust you.

INTRODUCTION
The Personal Is Political

Then they came for me
And there was no one left
To speak out for me.
Martin Niemöller[1]

There were other revolutionaries, for sure. Men who threatened the sovereignty of the kingdom. Men with followers into the thousands. But there was one whose threat surpassed the others. He not only threatened the rulers of his day but threatened those who deemed themselves protectors of the sacred. Of the superior. He challenged them. He revealed their flaws and called out their manipulations. And for that he would have to die. Well, for that, and so much more.

Jesus would hang on a cross for no other earthly reason than that he carried himself differently, spoke differently, and lived differently. And he did all this with an authority that should have belied a simple carpenter's boy from Nazareth. That difference would make him a target for all who felt empty and insecure in his presence. Whatever debates one might have about his divinity or the resurrection, one thing is abundantly, historically clear: Violence against his body would be the price Jesus paid for making men who'd thought themselves superior feel insecure.

1

This is a common thread in history.

The privileged have always protected their status by enacting violence in a myriad of forms against the poor, marginalized, and othered.

In America, the historical evidence of this is even more stark. David F. Krugler writes, "Between late 1918 and late 1919, the United States recorded ten major race riots, dozens of minor, racially charged clashes, and almost 100 lynchings as white Americans tried to enforce the continued subjugation of black Americans in the postwar era."[2]

So much of this violence boils down to one's perception—belief that one is greater than another because of gender (patriarchy) or sexual orientation (homophobia) or race (racism). And the acceptance of violence because of race is, in my opinion, the most insidious of these contentions because it's based on an incredible and rather blatant falsehood, a manufactured hierarchy, a construct built to protect class.

Michelle Alexander, in her book *The New Jim Crow*, outlines how notions of race supremacy or inferiority were carefully crafted:

> Nathaniel Bacon was a white property owner in Jamestown, Virginia, who managed to unite slaves, indentured servants, and poor whites in a revolutionary effort to overthrow the planter elite. . . . In an effort to protect their superior status and economic position, the planters shifted their strategy for maintaining dominance. . . . Fearful that such measures might not be sufficient to protect their interests, the planter class took an additional precautionary step, a step that would later come to be known as a "racial bribe." Deliberately and strategically, the

planter class extended special privileges to poor whites in an effort to drive a wedge between them and black slaves. White settlers were allowed greater access to Native American lands, white servants were allowed to police slaves through slave patrols and militias, and barriers were created so that free labor would not be placed in competition with slave labor. . . . Poor whites suddenly had a direct, personal stake in the existence of a race-based system of slavery.[3]

While it was true that these racial hierarchies had no bearing in reality, many an unscrupulous scientist has tried to create one. For example, in 1851, noted—albeit racist—physician Samuel A. Cartwright reported to the Medical Association of Louisiana, among other things, that "a Negro withstood the rays of the sun better because of an eye feature like one found in apes." He also claimed that "the black man's neck was shorter than a white person's, his 'bile' was a deeper color, his blood blacker, his feet flatter, his skull different."[4] These statements—firmly debunked—obviously weren't meant to humanize. Quite the contrary. They were designed to establish the supremacy of white people and justify the violence of enslavement and other types of subjugations. And yet here we are, forced hundreds of years later to defend the notion of race, of the Black-white binary, because of the violence perpetuated against those who are members of what some call the inferior race. Being Black, as a result of how white supremacy has injected its vile assumptions into every area and institution, is now very much a cultural reality—an identity forged in the midst of great pain and trauma, and one that must be defended as a means to access and maintain equity.

This manufactured distinction–turned–cultural reality has never been more pervasive than in these yet-to-be United States of America. Embedded in our DNA as a country, written into our Constitution, is the evidence of white supremacy. Article I, Section 2, of the U.S. Constitution blatantly states that, regarding representation in Congress, the enslaved African would be counted at three-fifths the value of white people—of lesser value politically.

And in the summer of 2020, during an unprecedented global pandemic, these heinous ideals reared their ugly heads, full and strong and fierce like a demented phoenix rising from the ashes of our pseudo-equality efforts. Overt violence returned to the forefront. Racial violence, while an ever-present reality in Black and Brown communities, is now a trending topic worthy of hashtags and *New York Times* think pieces. So much so that it's easy to become desensitized to what some have described as "trauma porn." I, too, grew numb to the headlines.

As someone who writes about race and faith and other "hot" topics, I'd grown accustomed to shutting down when the stories became too much. It was necessary for my mental and emotional health. There was always going to be another man like Philando Castile or woman like Breonna Taylor or boy like Tamir Rice or girl like Aiyana Stanley-Jones. People. Humans. All killed by someone who refused to see them.

Yes, shutting down was easy. Until it wasn't. Until the hashtags changed.

#Krogershooting

#JusticeforVickieLeeJones

On October 24, 2018, everything changed. My family was transformed forever by a level of hatred that I'd only really seen demonstrated on graphic internet clips and in the stories of my elders.

On a seemingly ordinary Wednesday, my elder cousin Vickie Lee Jones drove to her neighborhood Kroger grocery store and was shot dead in the parking lot by Gregory Alan Bush, who, according to witnesses, ended her life because she was Black. This was shortly after he'd shot and killed a grandfather, Maurice Stallard, who'd come to the store with his grandson to shop for school supplies.

I grew up in Jeffersontown, the suburb of Louisville where this horrific crime occurred. *That* Kroger is across the street from my parents' home. Bush had tried to enter my parents' church prior to shooting my cousin and Mr. Stallard when both Mom and Dad had just been there for Bible study an hour earlier. All of this means I've had to reckon with the fact that if something doesn't change soon, hate-crime shootings like the one that took these two precious lives, and all the innocent lives that came before and after, will be as commonplace as a daily social-media scroll through a millennial's life.

Hope is practically nonexistent when I think about the racist, xenophobic, patriarchal, oppressive dog-whistling that seems to come regularly now from those who call themselves our leaders. The oft-quoted poem by Martin Niemöller ends with "Then they came for me—and there was no one left to speak for me."[5] James Baldwin, in an open letter he wrote to activist and writer Angela Davis, co-signs this with, "If they come for me in the morning, they will come for you in the night."[6] It's a feeling that hides in my body. That one day it will be me. That one day it will be my child. That one day there will be no one left who will create my hashtag or say her name. That last line of Niemöller's poem resonates so much for me that it inspired the title of this book.

I know what will happen if we don't replace our reconciliation efforts with actual spiritual healing. More hate crimes will come. More of us will be desensitized to the pain. More hate will surely materialize if we don't actively stand against the oppression and suppression of Black and Brown people, women, LGBTQIA individuals, immigrants, and other marginalized groups. More hate is coming if we don't heal.

I wasn't the only one rocked by this proverbial storm. I'm part of a community of people, of family and friends, who were forever changed by the actions of one racist, white man. Just so the impact of racial violence is clear, I'd like to share a few words straight from the hearts of those closest to the victims.

> I was actually heading to work [that day]. Had been calling my mom for hours. When I got to work, I received a call from family members asking if I talked to my mom. After about 30 minutes of working, I got another call from my cousin saying I need to get over there. I informed my team leader and ran out to my car. I was about halfway to the Kroger from my job when my aunt called and told me my mom had been killed. I lost it in the car. Still not sure how I made it to the Kroger.
>
> I was very angry and confused. I punched a couple parking signs, crying until my eyes started hurting. If it wasn't for family members being there . . .
>
> Marcus Jones, youngest son of
> Vickie Jones and my cousin

That day was a regular, busy, and chaotic workday for me. In addition to the regular meetings, I also had a workforce recruitment event. That meant that the day before, I worked late and picked up my son from my parents' home later than normal. I was also attempting to get my son ready for a sleepover at his friend's home for the weekend and was trying to locate our sleeping bag. Throughout the day I was texting with my dad (as we normally did) about the sleeping bag situation, because of course he wanted my son to have what he needed and to help me by trying to do some things for me because my work schedule was so full.

In the afternoon, I was stressed and running late from a lunch meeting and trying to get to my office for another meeting. I was in my meeting, and my cell phone rang with a number I did not recognize, so I stopped the call and did not answer. Right after that it rang again, same number. . . .

"Excuse me, I need to take this call because someone is trying to reach me."

I answered and it was my son. My heart started beating really fast and I looked at my watch, because I thought that he should be with my dad. My dad picked him up from school for me. . . . His voice was different. He was crying, and anxious and scared. He said that Granddad had been shot. I remember saying, "Slow down, and repeat yourself." I heard him. I was just like, no, he is wrong. He said it again and said that he was shot in the back at Kroger. I remember jumping up and asking the person I was with to get the communications staff to see if something had happened at the Kroger.

I asked my son where he was and told him that I was coming. He was scared, crying, and the person who let him use the phone took the phone. She said that my son had run and was screaming and crying for help and had run to the Starbucks across the parking lot from the Kroger, and that she and her son had him. She asked where could they take him and I said I was downtown and on my way. I put her on hold and called my mother. I asked her if she had spoken with Dad, and she said no, he was picking up my son. I then told her what my son had told me. She was in disbelief just as I was. I combined the calls, gave the woman directions to my parents' home, and told them to stay on the line together until they got there. I then received a call on my work phone number from my supervisor, telling me that there was a shooting at that Kroger.

I then called my son's father [to meet us], and then my brother, who began checking hospitals. When I arrived at my parents' home, I hugged my son and tried to calm him. I then decided to go to the Kroger. My mother said she was coming with me. When we got there, people that I work with were there, waiting for me with some police officers I knew. Officers asked my mother what my dad was wearing when he left, and then the police chaplain walked up. I knew then. . . .

One of my good friends grabbed me as my legs went weak and hugged me. I was crying and screaming "NO!" over and over again. My other friend held my mother.

Later, my friend took my mother home, and I met my son and his dad at the police station. We sat

there for hours, waiting on a detective that special-
ized with children to interview my son. My cowork-
ers, my friends, were there with us, and no one left as
we waited.

Initially I was very confused and in protective
mode. I wanted to protect my child. I had never
heard him sound that way. His voice and that phone
call replay in my head all the time. I knew that I was
going to have to be rational and calm because I was
going to have to make decisions and I needed to find
out what happened. [Nevertheless], I physically felt
sick to my stomach and began to have a headache.

Kellie Stallard Watson, daughter of
Maurice Stallard and my sorority sister

On October 24, I was sitting at the bar, when the bar-
tender makes a vague statement saying that they are
getting wild in the area. I asked him what he meant
by that and he said, "They are shooting up at the
Kroger's." Knowing that my mother shopped there
all the time, I proceeded to call her but continually
got her voicemail. My sister-in-law and I were supposed to be heading to lunch, so when she called to
tell me she was ready, I asked her to swing through
that parking lot since she lived right by there. She
drives through and calls me back.

"Does your mom's car have a Louisville Cardinals
license plate on the front of it?"

I tell her yes and she says she sees the car, but
not Mom. I tell her that I am on my way. Five minutes later, I pull up in the Kroger gas station lot. My
sister-in-law said an officer told her that there had
been a shooting, and there were still people inside

the store giving interviews. Believing that Mom was one of the people being interviewed, we waited. Two hours later, my family pulls up. We all continue to wait and see when Mom is going to come out. More than an hour later, we see a group of people walking toward us. The coroner asks what we were there for and we inform him that we were waiting for my mother to come out from being interviewed in the store. He asked us her name and we tell him: Vickie Jones. He tells us she was one of the victims of the shooting. Needless to say, it took us by surprise and we were all upset. He proceeded to tell us that there were two victims. A gentleman inside the store, and my mother outside the store—fifty feet from where we were standing. They had covered her body, so we were unaware that she was even there. At this point, we are all upset and crying, but we notice all the news crews there with their cameras all pointing towards us.

Sean Jones, eldest son of Vickie Jones
and my cousin

I share, and will continue to share, these additional accounts beyond my own with you, in their own words, not just because the brunt of this kind of violence manifests differently in people, but also because it's important to demonstrate how the impact of racial violence is felt not just by the victims but whole families and communities. The heart-wrenching sound of one unarmed Black man crying out for his mother as a white police officer kneels on his neck reverberates well beyond those present or his family. That vibration reinforces the collective trauma that Black people have experienced for hundreds of years in this country. It challenges white people's understanding of their own capacity for empathy. It changes us all.

There were tears, of course. Plenty of those. And in moments where memories were shared, there were smiles and laughter. But there were stony faces also. Strong faces. Faces that stood resolute in the face of a horrific reality. As we laid my beloved cousin Vickie to rest, I was acutely aware of all the ways in which Black folks grieve, the ways in which we feel we have to hold our pain and move through the heartache that can come with constant dehumanization—the regular and consistent consciousness of how our bodies are not always safe in this world.

I've said it many times, but Black folks have to be the most resilient people on the planet. We certainly know how to "stand therefore" in the face of devastation as Scripture instructs (see Eph. 6:13–14). At least on the surface, where people can see, we see Black people reinventing ourselves so that we can navigate the sometimes painful experiences of this country and world. We unfortunately can be *too* good at this. We learn to bypass our pain. We allow the dominant culture to teach us that grinding away and being twice as good for half as much is a good thing. It isn't. It is a lie.

Resilience is certainly not a bad thing. It's kept generations of our people alive when slavery, Jim Crow, segregation, brutality, and daily dehumanization should have long killed us. I have a tremendous amount of grace for the way my ancestors chose to stay alive. But resilience comes at a cost. Resilience is making us sick.

As I've spent the last three years battling my own trauma-related health challenges, I've finally become resolute in one thing: I don't want to be sick anymore. Feeling grief and pain out loud is challenging. Some people don't understand it. They make assumptions about you when you are open about the things that hurt you and yours. But gratefully, I'm no longer invested or interested in the gaze of white folks, church folks, or any other kind of folks. I will cry sometimes because I know that my tears are cleansing. I will rage sometimes because I know anger that grows too big in a soul will burn it from the inside out. I will scream sometimes because somebody needs to hear my voice. This is also why I wrote this book. That's why I choose healing over reconciliation any day.

In John 5, Jesus asked a man laying at the side of the healing pool of Bethzatha, laying right *beside* the place that could heal his pain, "Do you want to be well?"

I ask the same of both white and Black readers. Are you ready to be well? What if wellness lives on the other side of pain and grief? What if wellness looks like sitting in the discomfort of what privilege and violence have wrought your fellow man? What if resilience isn't about pushing aside your trauma or the trauma you and your ancestors have caused but is more about sitting still enough to observe it—not maneuvering around it but moving through it? What would happen if Black folks released the need to show white folks that they can't hurt us, that they can't beat us? What if white folks released the need to pander and placate when plain old reckoning would do?

The remedy offered to those grieving, or anyone who has dealt with any kind of trauma, is to ground ourselves in the current moment. Being present means we aren't mired in the past, in the event that changed our lives, but it also means that we aren't required to think about a future so violently at odds with the one we'd imagined for ourselves. That latter piece is what's really important, because the truth is that we all have a vision for our lives. We all think about what we want and how things are supposed to go. And even if we come from the worst backgrounds or we've had the most traumatic childhood experiences, many of us still hold on to a little bit of hope that things will pan out the way they're supposed to. And so when we are faced with such overwhelming evidence to the contrary, violence that numbs us, it leaves us discombobulated. It becomes easy to focus on all the things we feel like we lost, all the things that are no longer possible. I'm never going to see my cousin Vickie, who I called Aunt Vickie because that's one way Black folks are taught to respect our elders, at the next family reunion or get-together. I will forever regret all the times I could have visited and didn't. I will no longer hear my mother talk about running into her at the Kroger across the street, the Kroger where she needlessly died. It's really easy for me to be deeply frustrated by what can't be, so choosing to focus on the present moment gives me an opportunity to not have to wrestle with what can never be anymore.

Which brings me to why I've written this book. I'm not an authority on grief. I just live with it daily. Part of being grounded in the present for me now means accepting it as a part of my journey on this plane. I used to think the work of my life was being a storyteller who centered and amplified the lived experiences of Black people. And while that's certainly a huge part of who I am and what I do, I now know that the work of my life is much more profound: finding ways not only to heal from the traumas this life and these systems have presented to me but also to maybe, hopefully, help someone else heal too. This book is honestly a chance to use all that I have learned, every emotion I've felt in these last few years, to speak out for those who may not know that their day is coming also.

Chapter 1
WHY BLACK TRAUMA MATTERS
We will heal through our breath.

What they don't tell you about this kind of grief, the kind born from inexplicable and unforeseeable violence, is that it consumes you. It grows roots in you, grounding itself into your being and bearing blue fruit—everything you say and do and feel is tinged and tainted with its presence. It is a shape-shifting thing, contorting and distorting itself to fit the shape and state of your soul. There is no time to breathe the way you should because the waves crash too fast. There's no time to right yourself before another overwhelms you. There's no way to anticipate the storm when it suddenly moves in. You are viciously smacked around inside by the realization that because of the skin you're in, you are not safe.

You are steeped in the awareness that one day you could be sitting in your home, drinking your tea, and thinking of ways to serve your sick mother. You could land on making her a meal and dropping off the platter to her nursing home room. You know it will brighten her day and you live to do just that. You could run to the Kroger grocery store around the corner to maybe pick up some cabbage because you know that she loves cabbage and you know how to make it just the way she likes it—fried with onions and whatnot. But there is something else. You could learn that you've won a murderous lottery. You could learn that you are the wrong color to be grocery shopping that day. You could find out that a white man with a gun has decided that today would be the day that you see the glory you always sang about in the choir. He has decided that you and another—a grandparent just like you—would have to pay for whatever is broken inside of him. You could pay with your life. And I imagine that you could lie there on the ground, next to your car, holding nothing but your trust in that glory beyond, as he stands over you—and you could hope that your mother and sons, your grandbabies and godchildren, your sisters and friends, and maybe even your little cousin who writes and writes and writes to exorcise the pain could eventually be all right.

We are not.

They don't tell you that this kind of grief feels grace-less. It attaches itself to other traumas and trials and complicates things. It devours any ridiculous notions of safe spaces and "There are good people in this world" and "Not all white men. . . ." This particular kind of grief, born from the insanity of racial violence, plays dodgeball with your spirit and no matter how quickly you move, how much you try to outthink it, it lands its hit every time. "You're out!" it announces to everyone around you before moving on to the next. And you are, you know. Out. In that moment when you are hit, you sit out until a new game starts, a new day with new mercies comes, and you can try again. As Solange sang, you can't dance it away, sex it away, drink it away, work this kind of grief away. You can't "look up dream houses on Zillow" it away.

You can't even write it away, though you will try. Oh, you will certainly try.

The history of trauma for Black Americans is as long as our time on these shores. It has, sadly, become part of our makeup. We are born with trauma woven into our DNA. It is the generational gift that keeps on giving. As children, it's hard to pinpoint where these innate feelings of insecurity might come from. It's hard to source our fears or apprehensions when we are little.

Much of what Black folks have intuitively felt in our bodies and understood in our minds has been confirmed by scholars. Vanessa Facemire stated in her dissertation, "Understanding the Insidious Trauma of Racism: An Exploration of the Impact of Racial Socialization, Gender, and Type of Racist Experiences," "Results indicated that experiences of racism (including individual, institutional, and cultural racism) are uniquely predictive of the endorsement of posttraumatic stress symptoms."[1] In "The Trauma of Racism," Lisa Firestone writes,

> In the United States, many black people are born into a life of trauma. It is a trauma informed by a long history of brutal inhumanity, repression, violence, and injustice that continues to firmly grip black men and women each and every day. This trauma is not something any of us who have not had the experience of being black in America can speak to in the same way as someone who has. Yet, acknowledging this trauma and casting it in a broad, unflickering light is all of our responsibility.[2]

In one of the most referenced works on the source and understanding of Black trauma, *Post Traumatic Slave Syndrome: America's Legacy of Enduring Injury and Healing*, Joy DeGruy contends, "Although slavery has long been

a part of human history, American chattel slavery represents a case of human trauma incomparable in scope, dura-
tion, and consequence to any other incidence of human
enslavement."[3]

The discussion of epigenetics—the study of how
experiences and environment can affect people on a genetic
level and be passed on generationally—is something that
is sprinkled throughout this book although maybe not in
explicit scientific terms. The idea that Black people today
are living with the transgenerational implications of racial
violence and discrimination is something that has been
studied and confirmed in great detail. What I'd like to do,
however briefly, is to consider how epigenetic or transgenerational trauma as it relates to the perpetrating of racial
violence has impacted white people and caused them to
continue in the tradition of their own ancestors.

This incomprehensible experience of enslavement
cannot be divorced from the current conversation about the
present-day experiences of Black people in this country, no
matter how much people may want it to be. The history of
the enslaved in America is linked to the terroristic lynchings in the post-Reconstruction South, which is linked to
the Great Migration of Black people to the North and West
only to experience systemic blockades to success, which is
linked to redlining and other forms of housing discrimination, which is linked to criminalization and mass incarceration, which is linked to police brutality, which is connected
to my experience with racial microaggressions and violence
and the continued experiences of millions of Black people
across the nation. In a 2016 Black History Month event
held in Laguna Honda Hospital in San Francisco, DeGruy
emphasized that link and the challenge inherent in it: "We
are trying to heal from past wounds while we are trying to

heal from present wounds, so we don't heal. Significant life-threatening events alter genes. We need to be well for the generations to come."[4]

And of course, Black folks are told ad nauseam by both society and the church that the answer is simply to forgive. That some of this ever-present pain we feel is a result of us "holding on" to these events too long when they happen, never mind that it feels like they never *stop* happening. We're told that the Bible says, "Love covers a multitude of sins" (see 1 Pet. 4:8) and Jesus said, "Do not judge, and you will not be judged; do not condemn, and you will not be condemned. Forgive, and you will be forgiven" (Luke 6:37). Black folks shouldn't give up to the devil any real estate in our hearts and minds when it comes to the sins made against us by white people today or a hundred years ago, right? Why can't we just let it go? you ask.

Those are good questions, but not for the reasons some might think. First, there isn't a single group on this planet who is asked with such a lack of empathy and compassion to forget the devastation and brutalization of their ancestors the way Black and Indigenous people are asked to do so in this country. It would be rightfully appalling to suggest that Jews should not remember with grave respect and reverence the atrocities of the Holocaust. So much of the forgive-and-forget rhetoric has to do with erasing the history of Black people in this country so that we can never engage with the remnants and residue of that history. All that said, there absolutely *is* a process of healing that every Black person must go through in order to experience the kind of spiritual and psychological liberty that has yet to be made physically available to us. I'll talk more about that necessary healing journey in future chapters. But first it must be said that forgiveness without accountability creates a trauma chasm so wide and deep that the true answer for many of us who are "holding on to pain" is discharging this pain in ways that, on the surface, may not be acceptable or palatable to those asking us to do it.

It means marching and protesting.

It means calling people out and in.

It means challenging the status quo.

It means demanding accountability for racial violence in an unrelenting fashion.

On one extreme, it might even mean revolution.

I believe that Black folks must do everything possible to live with joy and love and hope: being unapologetically spirited in the celebration of our culture, honoring who we are and the resilience that's also weaved into the fibers of our being. At the very least, it means placing the weight of our pain right back into the laps of those who are causing it and calling for a reckoning the likes of which this country has never seen.

The larger problem exists in white people being unable or unwilling—or both—to deal with how both the legacy and current demonstrations of racism and white supremacy still infect them. Eschewing discomfort in favor of color blindness has had devastating effects on the ability of the church to dig up this deep-rooted sin at the source. If there has been a generational impact on Black people as a result of slavery, Jim Crow, and so on, then there has also been a generational impact on white people. White people internalize a loss of authenticity of humanity when the lie of white supremacy is either actively championed or silently supported. Prolific author James Baldwin once wrote, "White people in this country will have quite enough to do in learning how to accept and love themselves and each other, and when they have achieved this—which will not be tomorrow and will not be today and may very well be never—the Negro problem will no longer exist, for it will no longer be needed."[5]

The need for there to be a group of people who remains under one's foot does something to one's soul. The same demonic spirit that allowed for good, Christian white folks to smile, take pictures, and bring their children to the public lynchings of Black men and women is the same one that allowed that white man to shoot my cousin in the parking lot of a grocery store. It is also the same spirit that allows good, Christian white folks to be silent and therefore complicit when Black folks speak, scream, cry, and rage about the sociopolitical cages from which we can't seem to free ourselves. The gospel of Jesus Christ mandates that believers address the needs of those in pain and mourning. Scripture says, "Rejoice with those who rejoice; weep with those who weep. Live in harmony with one another; do not be haughty, but associate with the lowly" (Rom. 12:15–16). So one can only imagine how a Black Christian might feel when encountering white believers who refuse to unravel the bias that has clearly been intertwined in *their* own DNA.

Racial trauma, then, has a dual impact on all of our mental, emotional, and spiritual health. First and foremost, Black folks are dehumanized via daily encounters of racial microaggressions or exposure to overt forms of racial violence. We internalize both forms of violence and, in addition to current systemic inequities, suffer from an increase in every negative marker for health and wellness. Erlanger Turner, an assistant professor of psychology at the University of Houston–Downtown, shared this notion with Rochaun Meadows-Fernandez for her article, "The Little Understood Mental-Health Effects of Racial Trauma": "Racial trauma is experiencing psychological symptoms

such as anxiety, hypervigilance to threat, or lack of hope-
fulness for your future as a result of repeated exposure to
racism or discrimination."[6] Symptoms also can include a
general mistrust of white people—something that resonates
with me as I remember my mother's perfect side-eye whenever a white person, friend or not, was in proximity.

White folks either directly participate in the dehumanization or they are direct beneficiaries of systems that
perpetuate systemic inequities. Both of these direct and
indirect investments are violent and create a false sense of
superiority (whiteness), exacting a spiritual price for being
the common denominator in all that is disruptive in our
world (see colonization, slavery, domination, disregard for
climate change and environmental concerns, etc.). That
spiritual price is real. The soul degrades.

Venita Blackburn in *The Paris Review* captures
this well:

> In truth, everyone knows that tribalism, and the lie
> of racism, could be eradicated, but no one agrees on
> the method. The only real solution is vulnerability,
> and that is no easy choice. To give up whiteness is to
> become vulnerable, to confront the deep tears in the
> psyche gouged over generations, to see hate in the
> face of a loved one and name it and therefore open
> yourself up to being seen and ultimately touched.
> For most morally sound people who benefit from
> whiteness, there is a need to absolve oneself of guilt
> and responsibility. . . .
>   . . . It is not the marginalized people, the black and
> brown bodies under assault, who carry the burden
> of saving this nation; they carry only the burden of
> seeing the flames first. When I say "save the nation,"

remember that America was born in cardiac arrest. The great experiment has never truly risen to sustainable levels. The cognitive dissonance necessary to profit off of gruesome human suffering and yet remain happy is too great.[7]

Black trauma matters because it's often compounded. When a white person murders a Black person because of racial bias or overt white supremacy and their murder is made public via social media and our twenty-four-hour news cycle, something is triggered in our Black bodies. This trauma porn becomes its own addiction, and with every post and share, our souls are devastated. The part of our consciousness that remembers what happened long before our own births, the memories of our grandmothers and great-grandmothers, is activated because the emotions are familiar. If, like me, there are already other wounds and personal traumas that live there, then we are simply being injected with a new version of the same terror and anxiety.

Everything blurs together. We can't parse out the external from the internal. We can't divide the personal from the collective. Everything is personal. Everything is collective.

Kenneth Hardy in "Healing the Hidden Wounds of Racial Trauma" writes,

> Racial oppression is a traumatic form of interpersonal violence which can lacerate the spirit, scar the soul, and puncture the psyche. Without a clear and descriptive language to describe this experience, those who suffer cannot coherently convey their pain, let alone heal. The source of their hurt is often confused with distracting secondary symptoms ranging

from hopelessness to acting out behavior. Racial oppression is seldom seen as contributing to these difficulties, and discussions of race are dismissed as manufacturing excuses, justifying bad behavior. As with other forms of trauma, we ask the wrong question about struggling youth of color. Instead of asking "What is wrong with them?" we need to ask the trauma-informed question, "What has happened to them?"[8]

As the elders in the old, southern, Black Baptist church of my childhood used to say, "Lord, I'm a witness." In July 2019, my body fell apart. More specifically, I had a health event that caused me to experience extreme tremors, dizziness, pressure in my head and chest, and other complications. After multiple visits to the hospital and numerous tests, there were still very few answers to my challenges. An inner-ear diagnosis explained one symptom. Perimenopause explained another. There was evidence of many other illnesses, but nothing confirmed. However, one constant was this idea that my experience with trauma, past and immediate, impacted how well my body could manage and ultimately heal from whatever was happening physically.

I was forced to be still for nearly eight months. I took leave from teaching and literally spent most of my days in bed. Sometimes I'd get up and walk around my garden. When the wooziness wasn't too bad, I'd take a little bit of a walk. But the stillness was a shock to me emotionally, psychologically, and spiritually. I'd never before had an experience where I couldn't do anything—where I couldn't produce, I couldn't work. Honestly, it was very challenging in the beginning. I had to reckon with the fact that I had lived in such a way that I only found my value in my work. I thought I was only as "good" as what I produced—whether it was writing or teaching or running a business. But that constant drive to produce was the very thing creating stress in my body and putting me in the position I found myself. When your body says it's done, there's really nothing you can do about it.

Some of the grappling I had to do in order to accept my inherent value as a human being beyond my level of productivity was a function of the personal trauma I'd experienced in my life. As a survivor of sexual abuse and assault, I didn't know that I was worthy of just being. Somewhere in my subconscious I thought my value was inextricably linked to my performance. I danced a jig daily in order to receive even the bare minimum of validation, and that took its toll. But some of those beliefs extended beyond my personal trauma and were the fruit of messages about who I was as a Black woman that I had internalized. Scholarship confirms this notion of work equaling value that many Black and Indigenous folks have taken on and where those ideas originate. One study in particular, by social scientist Christopher DeSante, concludes that "work ethic matters differently for blacks and whites. Whites are rewarded more for the same level of work ethic, and blacks are punished more for the same perceived level of 'laziness.'"[9] This confirms what Black folks have always known. The prevailing mantra of most Black households when I was growing up, including my own, was this idea that we have to be twice as good to get half as much. It's something that's drilled into us from very early on. And so, fully embodying what it takes to get that "half" requires a level of productivity not often seen in other groups. That's certainly not to say that other groups don't work hard, because of course they do. But this idea that solely working hard equates to being valuable or worthy of sometimes even just the bare minimum of resources is deeply problematic.

It is all a holdover of the residue of the transatlantic slave trade and the genocide of Indigenous people on this land, when our value was absolutely equal to our ability to work. We were a commodity. We were currency. We were property. And because of that, it was ingrained in us that the more cotton or tobacco or rice or whatever we could pick the more valuable we were—not to mention the transition into the postslavery Reconstruction era, where our very survival depended on working harder, or the greater portion of the twentieth century when, in the Great Migration from South to North and West, we would toil in factories and other jobs for upward of eighteen hours a day with no union to place guardrails on our labor. When we consider the actual facts of our history in this hemisphere, then it makes sense why this idea of work being the sole measure of your identity was and is common.

After generations of hearing these messages, this mindset can't help but penetrate you—even in relative freedom. It gets inside of you. Your body is liberated, but there is still work to do for your mind to be free. And frankly, to this day, a human's value being associated with productivity is honestly what drives capitalist society—for Black and Brown folks especially. Our social and political systems depend on its worker bees. Our educational systems are structured to produce more worker bees than queens. Not everyone can be at the top, and the system is designed to ensure that most people can't even remotely fathom how to get there. It's probably the worst pyramid scheme around. It's one thing when you have to reckon with personal issues that create such a limiting mindset. It's another thing when your personal issues are confirmed by the whole of society.

One that says you, especially as a Black woman, do not deserve rest. You have to earn your balance and calm. And if you, as a Black person, are resting, then you are somehow lazy. The only options, it would seem, are either to fight against this stereotype by constantly hustling and striving, or to embrace the stereotype and let it define you.

Beyond my personal traumas, there was something already very much in me that said that if I don't work myself to the bone, then I will somehow be seen as a failure. By whom? I honestly don't know. And yet I very much do know.

Most of the people who could judge my performance to the extent that it would prove detrimental for me to not perform were predominately white folks. Diversity, equity, and inclusion efforts aside, the bosses, professors, editors, and others in authority who had veto power in my life were still mostly white. Needless to say, those eight months in 2019 when I had to sit in the discomfort of doing nothing and allow all those feelings of failure and inadequacy to come to the surface presented the hardest fight of my life. Like Jacob, I wrestled with my angels until I finally submitted this anxiety to God and allowed each belief to be shed from me.

At that point, I began the work of understanding that my very being, *our* very nature, is one that reflects the image of God. We are loved. We are worthy, and no amount of work we can or cannot do will change that fact. That experience clarified for me what Paul meant when he wrote about "renewing [the] mind" (Rom. 12:2). I had to overhaul something that felt like it was written in my genetic code just so the things that really mattered to me—being a mom and a partner, and writing the stories I wanted to tell—could flourish. The physical pain during this time was bad.

I thought I was going to die. But the psychological traumas that were brought to the surface because of my stillness felt ten times worse. It took one moment on an acupuncturist's table when all of it emerged within what I now jokingly refer to as the wail heard 'round the world.

When my acupuncturist hit a particular point on my collarbone with a needle as fine as frog hair, I soon learned that, yes, there was certainly something physical happening, but there was also something spiritually and mentally that needed release. I instantly wailed—loudly—when that needle struck. It was like my grief had been forced to the surface and a tidal wave of sorrow enveloped me. It was odd and embarrassing but also a relief. The acupuncturist, a Christian, simply prayed with me. She said it was common. She also said that if a traumatic event has occurred and that event is compounded by other events, the trauma can literally remain trapped in our bodies. All the personal and collective turmoil had been bubbling up in me, creating this perfect storm of physical problems.

I honestly think that most Black and Brown folks experience this confluence of both our personal stuff—our own pasts, the things we deal with every day—and what we carry inside from our ancestors as a result of the very real systemic racism and violence we encounter regularly. And I suppose what happens is that those two things come together and create this perfect storm of unique challenges. This is the reason why, when we call out, "Black Lives Matter," there's a kind of healing in making that distinction. Yes, of course, all lives matter, but there's a particularity in our experience that has to be addressed—maybe even just so that I can have the privilege of being able to deal with my personal stuff.

It's no coincidence that the upheaval of my health happened within a year of the murder of my cousin . . . after a particularly difficult year fighting for diversity and inclusion on the college campus where I teach . . . after writing about the murders of Botham Jean, Stephon Clark, and Atatiana Jefferson. One of the beauties found in the way God created us is how intricately connected our bodies, minds, and spirits are. Some of what we call "illness" and "disease" can be linked to how much personal and transgenerational trauma we hold in our bodies.

> Traumatized people chronically feel unsafe inside their bodies: The past is alive in the form of gnawing interior discomfort. Their bodies are constantly bombarded by visceral warning signs, and, in an attempt to control these processes, they often become expert at ignoring their gut feelings and in numbing awareness of what is played out inside. They learn to hide from their true selves.[10]

This affirmation by scientist Bessel van der Kolk in *The Body Keeps the Score* demonstrates why my physical challenges were likely linked to the trauma of not only my personal losses but my current work as a writer on subjects related to race and social justice. It reminds me of why the recognition of the collective trauma of Black people as a result of white supremacy and systemic racism is a necessary stop on the journey toward healing. True emotional liberty and spiritual liberty are ultimately at stake.

> The time came when the Lord God formed a man's body from the dust of the ground and breathed into

it the breath of life. And man became a living person.
(Gen. 2:7 TLB)

There were moments in 2019 when I was in so much pain,
so disoriented, that all I had was my breath. It was the only
thing I could count on. I centered my focus there because
no other part of my body could hold my attention without causing panic and tears and fears of dying. In those
moments of stillness, with every inhale and exhale, the tears
of not just forty-plus-year-old Tracey surfaced. The tears
of my inner nine-year-old were also caught in my breath.
At that point, I realized that, due to both personal and collective trauma, I'd been holding my breath longer than I
could remember. When I wanted to throttle back my emotions, keep any agony at bay, I would unconsciously hold
my breath, sipping just enough air to not pass out. Deep,
from-the-diaphragm inhales just weren't a thing for me.
And when I started breathing, truly breathing, my body
was often wrecked with an emotional tidal wave forty years
in the making.

    I suspect it's the same for many Black folks. Inun-
dated with images of physical racial violence, alongside the
daily awareness of the psychological violence of racial discrimination and microaggressions, many of us have learned
to hold our proverbial breaths. Otherwise the sorrow and
rage might overtake us. I also wonder if this is the reason
why the video of George Floyd being murdered by police
officer Derek Chauvin held us all so captive. We'd heard
Eric Garner cry out, "I can't breathe," years before, and
here it was again. Louder, more pronounced. A symbol of
what racial violence has done to all of us. Floyd's voice cried
out for his long-passed mother—a crying out to the womb
that held all his beginning. And then: the snuffing out, the

suffocation, the stealing of God's holy life force from that same voice. An ending. All of our individual and collective trauma cracking the surface of our notions of respectability, of "hanging in there" and "Black excellence." In the silencing of Floyd's breath, we exhaled all that we'd been holding in, and all heaven broke loose.

And still, I just want Black folks to breathe again, more, always.

One of the things that many white people don't want to contemplate or accept is that healing is not always nonconfrontational. The healing of Black and Indigenous people from racial violence and the trauma that is birthed from it nearly always requires accountability from those who either perpetrate or benefit from that violence. The full restoration of our collective breath will require a kind of reckoning from white folks—yes, even the most progressive—that is uncomfortable at best. It's not just the raised voices of protestors in the summer of 2020 that should be your clarion call. Just like the biblical Abel, killed by his brother Cain, the blood of my cousin and the blood of all the hashtagged men, women, and children—and even the blood of all the ancestors whose names we will never know—cry out for justice.

Chapter 2

IT'S ALL INTERSECTIONAL

*We will heal by recognizing the myriad of ways
the image of God is reflected in us.*

I watch the moving image flash across the screen with a
kind of intense wonder. My daughter, five years old at the
time, is dancing freely in the middle of a crowd at the annual
Odunde street festival in Philly. She is twisting and twirl-
ing with abandon, not caring one bit about what the people
beside or in front of or behind her are thinking. She's not
afraid that she will be told to stop or made to feel like she
is too much. She simply hears the enticing rhythms of the
Afrobeats music playing on the loudspeakers on South
Street and lets it take her into her own world.

I hit refresh and watch it again.

And again.

Tears fall fast. By the fifth time I watch the clip, my
face is soaked.

She is free. For now.

I am emotional because it dawns on me that this is
what liberation looks like on my beautiful, brown baby girl.
My heart lurches with a mixture of joy and sadness. Joy
because I've had the honor of providing her with the space
to be so free, to not have to be concerned with the ways the
world will ultimately, eventually see her. Sadness because
every day I anticipate the moment when it will all change.
She's ten now—living in a global-pandemic, post–Breonna

Taylor world. Her light has not been put out completely, but it has certainly dimmed significantly since that day at the festival. It makes me wonder what will happen at thirteen. Certainly, by the time she is fifteen, life as a young Black girl in America will have shifted. *Will liberty still be within her grasp?* The intersection of being both Black and a woman will likely have revealed what this country—white folks, in particular—see when they look at her. In some cases, she will be seen as a threat (Rekia Boyd), even when she herself is in crisis (Natasha McKenna and Michelle Cusseaux). Her questions will be deemed too uppity, haughty even (Sandra Bland). Assumptions will be made about her lifestyle and choices of partner that might render her unworthy of even sleeping in peace (Breonna Taylor). Standing her ground against the violence that feels inevitable, a right touted as allegedly necessary by white conservatives, won't likely be afforded to her (Korryn Gaines).

"Intersectionality" is such a buzzword nowadays that I hesitate to even use it because it seems to be one of a long list of concepts that some white Christians immediately denounce without a clear understanding of what it means, or even if they do acknowledge that it exists, they don't seem to be very interested in digging into how it shows up in the lived experiences of the marginalized people who give the word its existence. That said, even when the white gaze is present, it's never my priority and so I choose to forge ahead. Scholar and activist Kimberlé Crenshaw's work on intersectionality, a term she coined more than thirty years ago, is an incredible guide to understanding how patriarchy and misogynoir show up in our churches and mission work and fuel the racial violence from which other Black folks and I are healing.

Intersectionality is a firmly defined concept. In an interview with *Columbia Law News*, Crenshaw offers clarity on what the theory means: "Intersectionality is a lens through which you can see where power comes and collides, where it interlocks and intersects. It's not simply that there's a race problem here, a gender problem here, and a class or LGBTQ problem there. Many times that framework erases what happens to people who are subject to all of these things."[1]

In light of the concept being such a lightning rod nowadays for many who have not done the work to understand it, I think it might be important to talk a bit about what intersectionality is not. So many people see the injection of intersectionality in the discourse as a kind of reverse racism or a way for those with multiple identities to take advantage of a system they believe is working perfectly. Yet Crenshaw's work clearly indicates that it is not about flipping the current racial hierarchies or giving marginalized groups the ability to "oppress the oppressors," but more about investigating and dismantling deep systemic inequities. Yes, our systems—political, legal, social, educational, and economic—*are* working perfectly. They are working the way they were designed to work when this country was founded in 1776 and people who look like me would have been enslaved. Investigating the way an already biased system affects those with multiple marginalized identities—with an eye toward dismantling it—is what an intersectional lens does. If you're someone who is hit by these systems at every angle, facing potential discrimination and increased violence because you are, say, both Black and a woman, you probably aren't terribly focused on getting *more* than you deserve. It's about justice and equity. It's about all of your identities having a say in how you respond to certain kinds of treatment.

If I say that, as a Black woman, I face very specific kinds of violence that are different from other groups, that is in no way taking away from the violence Black men or white women face or the violence Black trans and non-binary people face. What I'm actually saying is that my particular intersection has value and is experiencing this *thing* in a very different way, a way that needs investigation. What I also might be saying is that because I am a Black woman, the violence against me looks different and, in many cases, is compounded. My experience is different than if one of the "roads in my intersection" is a privileged identity that meets the social standard by which every other identity is unfortunately measured. For Black men, being a man is still viewed to be the standard in our mostly patriarchal world, so the maleness of their identity is not likely what creates violence for them. It's the Blackness and all its associated stereotypes, biases, and fears. But if you add another marginalized identity—say, being a queer Afro-Latina over sixty years of age—then the theory of intersectionality says that the potential for discrimination and violence is greater. Every single time I add an identity that is not the standard, I run the risk of experiencing more violence as a result of that additional marginalized identity.

I know that people see me differently not just because I'm Black, but also because I'm a Black woman—and even more so because I'm a Black woman who has already been touched by racial violence of the worst kind. It's obvious in the way people engage with me. Before my code-switching button permanently broke, I used to sit in job interviews, dressed in what I was taught to be appropriate corporate attire—a blue suit, stockings, hair straightened—and the conversation I'd have with the person interviewing me would tell me very clearly that, one, they did not expect for me to be a Black woman when I walked through the door. And two, what they expected me to sound like or say or do was very clearly connected to their own personal biases of who Black women are. When they couldn't box me in, they, in many cases, made decisions about my viability, about whether I was a good fit for their company culture despite checking off the boxes on paper and based on nearly nothing of what I actually said in the interview. I know this because I've seen the other side. I've seen hiring committee members in academia vocalize these assumptions. I've also been hanging out with friends in college, doing what college kids do, and watching police officers or other white people in authority seem to be champing at the bit just waiting for me to pop off because that's who they believed Black women to be. To be clear: "popping off" was a euphemism for anything that seemingly challenged their authority, including asking a question that is totally within my right to do so. This was and is especially hurtful, considering that on more than one occasion, the repercussions for some of the white women I'd observe on campus "mouthing off" were significantly less detrimental or violent.

This inequity often sparks the immediate desire to find exception in the cases involving women who look like me. Sandra Bland, Korryn Gaines, and Breonna Taylor all seem to have had both their Blackness and their womanness wielded against them in ways that white women do not (this is really the birthplace of the controversial "Karen" moniker, which ultimately is a way to name the person who gets away with this behavior). Even as much as Black men are seen as causing their own deaths in their violent encounters with police—not allowed to make human moves (removing a wallet because they were asked for ID) or mistakes (running away out of fear, loitering while intoxicated) without the penalty of death, Black women are even more likely to experience extreme accountability not just for our actions but for the actions of others against us. Black men should not have resisted, should not have run, should not have moved too quickly or committed that petty crime that would have gotten a white man a slap on the wrist or a week in jail. Black women also should not have resisted, should not have run, but the special misogynistic sauce is that we are also blamed for supposedly being, by our very nature, provocative. We "caused" the cop, the person, whoever to respond to us that way. We made the police officer sexually assault us (the most pervasive form of violence against women of color by law enforcement) because of what we wore or how we presented ourselves. *Black women are sex fiends.* We made the man kill us because we defended ourselves too loudly. *Black women are naturally too bold and loud.* LaShawn Harris writes in "#SayHerName: Black Women, State-Sanctioned Violence & Resistance," "Drawing from turn-of-the-twentieth-century racist and sexist caricatures and Black crime statistics, state and federal lawmakers and enforcers mounted derisive attacks against women and girls, identifying them as anticitizen, pathological and hypersexual, and as moral and legal threats to American civilization."[2]

So yes, the differences between some of the violence wielded against Black men as opposed to Black women are slight. The line is so gray, but it's still there. Black women should not have driven with a broken taillight and should have used our words to soothe the officer instead of further inflaming him. Being a woman means we trigger not just white men's potential racial biases but also their sense of patriarchal importance. *How dare this Negro woman stand up for herself?*

Even in discussing police abuses of power and state-sanctioned violence, what Black women experience is distinctly different from what Black men may experience. But to be clear: there's no hierarchy. This isn't the oppression Olympics. I would never imply that one is somehow worse than the other. Violence of any kind is deeply traumatic. That said, however, the experience of Black women is distinct because it's often not seen. Our experience with violence doesn't often end with death and therefore is often overlooked. As Michelle S. Jacobs writes in "The Violent State: Black Women's Invisible Struggle against Police Violence," "Black women are subjected to every type of law enforcement violence imaginable. The most severe violence causes death, but Black women are routinely brutalized by the police in ways that do not cause death."[3]

And even when it does, there are myriad reasons why people aren't necessarily moved to action in the same ways as they are for Black men.

George Floyd's horrific murder at the hands of police officer Derek Chauvin in May 2020 triggered a racial outcry and unrest that hadn't been seen since the early 1990s. Breonna Taylor's murder, equally horrifying for different reasons, happened two months prior and didn't have the same impact. In fact, it wasn't until after the videos of both Ahmaud Arbery's and George Floyd's murders hit the internet that the cries to *also* say Breonna Taylor's name hit a fever pitch. But she wasn't the catalyst for the movement. Whether we are talking about LaJuana Phillips or Tanisha Anderson, we are sadly never the catalyst. Crenshaw, who is also the founder of the African American Policy Forum and creator of the 2014 #SayHerName campaign, weighed in on this: "[Breonna Taylor's case] could have easily been forgotten, and it was almost forgotten . . . but I think the fact that other cases were happening in the same season made it harder to simply overlook her case."[4]

Again, this isn't a competition. There are no awards for whose violent racial experience will galvanize the world. Whichever loss creates change for all of us is devastatingly fine. But I do think that making these distinctions is important if we want to examine how violence shows up intersectionally—if we want to create a kind of consciousness or awareness about what's happening to specific groups and shift the way we think about them and their experiences on a day-to-day basis.

Whenever I'm writing about race or racial reconciliation, and intersectionality in particular, I return to the opening passages of John 4. They always resonate with me and reveal so much about the way Jesus modeled engaging with the so-called other—particularly the way we should engage people who are racially or ethnically different from us. Consideration of the ways in which identities are intersectional and come with both discrimination and violence is a cornerstone of the compassion that Jesus showed when he engaged the woman at the well—knowing full well that her status as both a Samaritan and woman warranted disregard by him, a Jewish rabbi.

> [Jesus] left Judea and returned to Galilee.
> He had to go through Samaria on the way. Eventually he came to the Samaritan village of Sychar, near the field that Jacob gave to his son Joseph. Jacob's well was there; and Jesus, tired from the long walk, sat wearily beside the well about noontime. Soon a

Samaritan woman came to draw water, and Jesus said to her, "Please give me a drink." He was alone at the time because his disciples had gone into the village to buy some food.

The woman was surprised, for Jews refuse to have anything to do with Samaritans. She said to Jesus, "You are a Jew, and I am a Samaritan woman. Why are you asking me for a drink?"

Jesus replied, "If you only knew the gift God has for you and who you are speaking to, you would ask me, and I would give you living water."

"But sir, you don't have a rope or a bucket," she said, "and this well is very deep. Where would you get this living water? And besides, do you think you're greater than our ancestor Jacob, who gave us this well? How can you offer better water than he and his sons and his animals enjoyed?"

Jesus replied, "Anyone who drinks this water will soon become thirsty again. But those who drink the water I give will never be thirsty again. It becomes a fresh, bubbling spring within them, giving them eternal life."

"Please, sir," the woman said, "give me this water! Then I'll never be thirsty again, and I won't have to come here to get water." (John 4:3–15 NLT)

John 4:4 stands out to me because Jesus is returning to Galilee from Judah. Before we even meet the Samaritan woman, we must acknowledge that Jesus *has* to go through Samaria—the foreign place, the home of people who are looked down on by the Jews. In order for Jesus to get where he has to go, he has to go through a place where people are different. He has to encounter the marginalized people of his

day. I challenge people who have allowed white supremacy
to embed itself so deeply inside them that they don't even
recognize how they act out in ways that support this infra-
structure to realize that in order for you to get where you
truly need to be, you're going to have to encounter people
who are different. There is something glorious on the other
side of navigating relationships with people who are racially
and ethnically different from you.

So, from the start, I think this passage is really teaching us about the nature of what those kinds of encounters
may be. Just a few verses down, the woman who is surprised
that Jesus is asking her to give him a glass of water straight
up says, "You are a Jew, and I am a Samaritan woman."
She is acknowledging her intersections! It's not even just
about her being a Samaritan, but it's also about her being
a woman. The crossroads of patriarchy and ethnicity, and
the isolation and discrimination that come along with them
are clear. Samaritans are like the not-so-long-lost cousins
of the Jews, and yet a grand disconnect exists between the
two cultures.

Then something powerful happens. The woman
essentially says, "Why are you—one of the ones who believe
yourself to be superior—asking me for a drink?" What we see
here is a dynamic exchange of physical resources for spiritual resources. One of the critiques of the Western church
has been the disconnect that sometimes exists between serving someone's physical needs versus serving their spiritual
needs. Serving someone's physical needs doesn't just show
up in soup kitchens and clothing drives. It's also about figuring out how to dismantle systems of poverty and educational disparities that often make those kitchens and drives
necessary. And serving someone's spiritual needs doesn't
just include preaching sermons every Sunday. We can talk

about Jesus until we're blue in the face, but you can't disconnect the tangible work of dismantling systemic racism
from the work of tending to someone's spirit. Later on in
Scripture, we read, "Hey, if someone is hungry, feed them"
(see Jas. 2:14–16). Don't come to people with your tracts
and notions of Jesus as savior if you're not willing to be a
vessel through which their physical needs are met. And *my*
physical needs are more than just food and water. One of my
physical needs is feeling safe enough to walk into a grocery
store without wondering if I will be shot because I'm Black.

On the one hand, the exchange of physical for spiritual resources in this story balances out the power differen-
tial between Jesus and this woman. The reciprocity here is
so powerful. It's Jesus asking for his own physical need to
be met. He's weary. He's tired. He's sitting by Jacob's well
and he's thirsty. And this person has the capacity to serve
him. She can draw from that well. She has the bucket. She
has the rope. He does not. Jesus recognizes that she has
something of value to offer him. She is the privileged one in
that scenario when it comes to the physical need. She can
draw some water for him, but in exchange he offers what he
is privileged to give—living water, a spiritual filling.

This stands in stark contrast to the very skewed, colo-
nizing, missionary mindset of many white Christians. They
go into places and communities under the guise of bringing
the good news of Jesus. They bring food they themselves
wouldn't eat and clothes they wouldn't wear, oblivious to
the systemic causes of the physical needs that exist in the
community. They fail to see anything of value in those communities already, a blessing for them waiting in the midst of
the people the white Christians are claiming to save. This
view disregards the real possibility that Jesus may already
be there, just not in a form they recognize. Many white

Christians assume they are bringing the living water into those spaces rather than being positioned to receive it.

I also love that the Samaritan woman makes no bones about challenging the theology that Jesus' ethnic background represents. He is a Jew. And so she, in verse 20 (NLT), very clearly asks, "So tell me, why is it that you Jews insist that Jerusalem is the only place of worship, while we Samaritans claim it is here at Mount Gerizim, where our ancestors worshiped?"

She goes *in*, and I'm here for it!

That difference in the locus of worship was central to Jews' prejudice against Samaritans. Similarly, there is often an intense scrutiny among white Christians of the way that Black folks use language, imagination, lived experience, and movement in our worship—everything from denouncing Black liberation theology to completely disregarding womanist interpretations of Scripture. This is likely based in the belief, especially in Western evangelical circles, that there is a particular way to worship, a particular set of rules that one needs to follow. Danté Stewart, author of *Shoutin' in the Fire: An American Epistle*, wrote on Twitter,

> If people in the Hebrew Bible can imagine God as a sun and shield, then black people can imagine God as black and, as Alice Walker writes, the Ultimate Ancestor. If people can have the imagination to see Aslan [from the Chronicles of Narnia] as representative of Jesus, then there should be no problem when black women say that the experience of God and faith is found in "our mother's gardens." But sadly, many can see the symbol of divine goodness and revelation in an animal, an object, and in whiteness before they can ever see the symbol of divine goodness in black

life, black literature, and the black world. Theologian M. Shawn Copeland is right: this theology is
harmful and must be decolonized. Our theology, as
Baby Suggs preaches in Toni Morrison's *Beloved*,
should make us "love what you have been taught not
to love." If we have been taught this way, we can be
taught another.[5]

Jesus clears this up for all of us by essentially saying,
"Yeah, there have been these rules. However, there's going
to come a time when none of it will matter. It's going to
only matter whether you worship in spirit and in truth" (see
John 4:21–22).

Listen, we can't parse that out or pretend like we
didn't read it. We can't sit here and say, "Oh, but what he
meant was. . . ." No. It's very clearly stated here, whether
you're taking a literal or a metaphorical lens to this passage,
that these divisions, these lines, have been drawn by man
and not God. And what I love more about this part of their
interaction is that he's not moved at all by her challenge.
He's not writing a blog post trying to justify the Jewish traditions and tearing down this "postmodern perspective"
she has. And he's certainly not withholding his love. He's
not withholding his insight. He's not withholding his attention from this woman because she challenged him. The
engagement continues. There is a conversation. There is
a discussion. If we believe that Jesus is both human and
divine, then we know that he is aware of what's happening
in that moment. He is aware of what's going on in her mind
and heart; the glorious alchemy that he wields is transform-
ing her in real time. And what I find even more telling is
that after she leaves and tells the townspeople what she
heard from the Messiah, the disciples return, and they are

so "shocked" by the sight of Jesus talking to the woman that they can't actually see the exchange that has occurred. He sets them straight, though.

> Just then his disciples came back. They were shocked to find him talking to a woman, but none of them had the nerve to ask, "What do you want with her?" or "Why are you talking to her?" The woman left her water jar beside the well and ran back to the village, telling everyone, "Come and see a man who told me everything I ever did! Could he possibly be the Messiah?" So the people came streaming from the village to see him.
>
> Meanwhile, the disciples were urging Jesus, "Rabbi, eat something."
>
> But Jesus replied, "I have a kind of food you know nothing about."
>
> "Did someone bring him food while we were gone?" the disciples asked each other.
>
> Then Jesus explained: "My nourishment comes from doing the will of God, who sent me, and from finishing his work." (John 4:27–34 NLT)

For white people who call themselves allies, you inevitably will have to wrestle with the people who see you listening and changing and advocating. You will have to deal with people in your space who will say, "What are you doing? Why are you talking to that person? We don't do that." Or maybe, like the disciples, they don't have the nerve to say it aloud. They will find other ways to express their concern about your white son dating a Black woman or your standing lunch date with the coworker from Ghana. I suppose they are entitled to their feelings. But know what

Jesus knew. Your fulfillment and your spiritual nourishment come from doing the will of God. And I can't imagine that God's will would not include you acknowledging the sin of white supremacy and lovingly engaging with another person as an equal.

There's another lesson here. As Black folks deal with the pain of racial violence, something about the power of relationships is healing. Engaging with each other within our community, as well as with those outside of it who are willing to expose and lay aside their racial biases, is most certainly a kind of nourishment. If we as Christians claim to live lives modeled after the Christ, then it makes sense to consider the ways in which Jesus acknowledges this Samaritan woman's intersections; he likely knew full well that women gather water at the well, the geographic location meant that it would likely be a Samaritan woman, and the time of day suggests that he knew she was somewhat of an outsider in her community, at best. Yet he engaged her, viewing her worthy of words, time, attention, and his gift of living water. He didn't patronize her. He didn't even try to "save" her in the ways we see people from dominant cultures try to save those they believe are different or not aligned with their standard. He simply offered her something she'd likely never seen or felt before—his acknowledgment and spiritual refreshment.

We see the very opposite of this scenario in the way that intersectionality shows up in how Black and Brown women are treated by law enforcement or other forms of given or assumed authority by mostly white men. We are victims of brutality, some of which seems to be state-sanctioned. How we are treated, how the cases of brutality against us are framed by the media, are all part of the violence. Yes, even the media framing is violence; consider the choices of photos or headline language used to depict and describe victims—something I discuss more in a later chapter. When stereotypes and racial biases are used to create a narrative of who Black and Brown women are, it is dehumanizing. As writer Chimamanda Ngozi Adichie has said, it creates a single story of us.[6] We become the single story of our intersecting identity instead of human beings living and learning and, yes, experiencing the same reasonable consequences for mistakes as our white counterparts.

The bottom line? Violent and traumatic things happen specifically to Black women because we are both Black and women—things that don't happen in the same ways to white men, white women, or even Black men. This is never more clearly demonstrated than in the church.

The church already has an issue with patriarchy. We've twisted Scripture verses that talk about household leadership in a very specific cultural context into tenets in favor of male dominance and superiority (see Eph. 5:22–6:9 and Col. 3:18–4:1). I grew up in a church where women not only couldn't preach from the pulpit but couldn't even step foot in the pulpit. Doing so was such an egregious error that it sometimes garnered extreme verbal reprimands. This also meant that in order to get to the other side of the choir stand, we had to walk down the stairs or all the way behind the pulpit area as opposed to the shortest route through it. Church "nurses" were required to lean over into the pulpit from the back choir stand rows in order to change out the pastor's water glasses—again, instead of doing what would make the most sense (and stop a lot of excess water from hitting the floor) by simply walking over to the chair and changing the pitcher. Nothing about that was godly, nor scriptural. That patch of red velvet carpet was not the Holy of Holies by any stretch. This rule simply served the patriarchal traditions that had been in place for years and highlighted the male leadership's seeming need for control. Sure, no one died because of this, but it was violence just the same. For many girls growing up in that environment, it taught us that our very presence could be unholy, that we automatically taint or diminish a place by virtue of our womanhood. Church then ceases to be a safe place for other women and me. The impact of this experience is exacerbated by society's determination that the color of our skin also automatically taints a space.

So even what we see in the church has created a transgenerational trauma response for us that often requires therapy interventions that are not always accessible to many. In fact, maybe the reason we see internalized misogyny in the church is that women in general, and Black women specifically, *know* we won't be protected.

I always find it fascinating when people question the validity of intersectionality or especially when Christians, white Christians specifically, find problems with it. I've had numerous white Christians approach me and say rather explicitly that intersectionality is not a thing because once we become believers our only identity is found in Christ. They believe we have no other identity and should operate as such (as if Jesus himself, or even the apostles, weren't acutely aware of their identity as Jews within the Roman Empire). It's also ironic because the way God is presented in most traditional contexts is itself an imperfect (and problematic, for some) intersectional perspective. The Trinity, this theological concept that there is one sovereign, divine entity that shares multiple identities (Father, Son, and Holy Spirit)—identities that often intersect—is something that many Christians are taught to embrace wholesale.

Even more fascinating is the fact that the way these identities interact with each other impacts other people. We only have to look as far as the Gospels and Jesus' relationship with the Father to find confirmation of this.

So evidently, resistance to intersectionality has nothing to do with the concept itself. People are often being obtuse when they suggest that it's a core disagreement with the theory. I'd argue that the challenge is often with *who* is presenting these ideas and how they are being utilized as a means to establish equity—that's really the basis of the fight against intersectionality, Critical Race Theory, and so on. The belief persists that the pursuit of equality or equity for Black people means that something has to be taken away from white people, and there is some truth to this. Acknowledging intersectionality as well as the deep physical and psychic wounds caused by racism means that white folks will lose—wait for it—their conscious and unconscious notions of superiority, their sense of entitlement over spaces occupied by people who don't look like them. Sadly, however, racial violence, especially in the form of "law and order," is often enacted to ensure that equity is never fully actualized and white supremacy is maintained. This saddens me, especially when I know that so many who claim Jesus as Lord and sincerely believe that he has called us to love our neighbors as ourselves can't or don't care to conceptualize how dehumanizing this kind of willful ignorance is.

Embracing the myriad ways that God's image is reflected in every human on earth is the clear starting point toward healing. We often say we believe in the *imago Dei* (the idea that humans are made in the image of God), but do we know what that really means? God said in Genesis, "Let us make humankind in our image" (Gen. 1:26). (Note the "us" and "our," reflecting that intersectionality of being.)

We interpret this as meaning that everything in creation reflects the divine. White supremacy, then, is diametrically opposed to this central tenet of our faith. And when it comes down to the very tangible ways that the *imago Dei* shows up in our lives, well, it means accepting me—in all my identities—as someone who's made in the image of God and not accepting the ways I've been treated by individuals and institutions that negate that image.

But this requires a capacity for vulnerability that many white people cannot access. It means reflecting on one's own participation in this kind of dehumanization, whether by virtue of being silent in the face of violence, indirectly benefiting from discrimination against Black and Indigenous people and other peoples of color, or directly punching down. One will have to be honest about whether they truly believe that Black and Brown people are equally made in the image of God and deserving of all the things that God has for us as human beings in all the same ways that they believe this about themselves.

It's really telling when white Christians are confronted with this and, as a Black person, you can feel their dissonance. Inevitably what follows is a kind of false righteousness, a take-my-ball-and-go-home boundary setting that tells me that they are unable to reckon with the feelings that have arisen in them. Entitlement rears its ugly head, which is followed by all the reasons Black and Brown people shouldn't have access to the same things as them. I imagine that the internal conviction one might experience when confronted with what they really feel about another human being is what drives all the faulty explanations about why Black people don't live in their neighborhood or are unable to obtain a bank loan for a small business or, yes, are shot and killed for running a red light.

Whether in secular environments and institutions or in the church, it's really a kind of audacity of whiteness that believes that my humanity or my *imago Dei* can be stolen from me anyway. I get that because it is so woven into our social and political systems that this power feels real. It certainly feels real to every Black mother and father who has to bury a child because of racial violence. But it's not. You can kill us, but you can't *kill* us.

Some of the ways intersectional racial violence shows up became clearer with the murder of my cousin. I have always understood the disparities, and I've written about them time and time again. But my own personal connection to that difference, to that disparity, became evident.

I don't think I really understood just how much being Black and a woman shifted the way people perceive me or my daughter or any other women and girls in my life, how exposed we personally were to those who would perpetrate racial violence against us. I didn't realize just how much I unconsciously shift the way I move through the world— even how I engage my own faith—because of it.

When my cousin was murdered, I was terrified. I stopped going to grocery stores. After years of saying no, I finally thought that maybe it *would* be good for us to have a legal firearm to protect our home. I can't necessarily say that my cousin's murder was specifically because of her being both Black and a woman. I don't know how much gender played a role in it. But at the same time, when I look at all of the other stories, I can't help but wonder. The shooter, Gregory Bush, also came across Dominiic Rozier, a Black man, that day. That man was armed with a gun he was licensed to carry and exchanged gunfire with Bush after he'd killed my cousin Vickie and pointed a gun at Dominiic's wife. I can't help but wonder if my cousin's helplessness or seeming defenselessness, because of age and gender, made a difference.

All I know is that I move through the world differently now. As a Black woman from the South who has been sexually assaulted, I'd always been hyperaware. But something shifted for me in October 2018. As "woke" as I believed myself to be, I felt that, in that moment, I had reached another level of awareness. So much of the violence that Black women experience doesn't often end in death and therefore is not viewed as "just as bad." But when it does end in death, the violence is like a cancer that metastasizes through whole families and communities in the form of trauma. This thing I carry in me now, that I go to therapy for and I pray to heal from, is something that's probably going to stay with me until I leave this earth. And while there is certainly a devastation and finality to death, to have to live with this trauma feels like the most frightening thing about racial violence in general, and specifically racial violence that happens to women.

So to be clear: not only do I move through the world differently as a Black person, but I move differently as a woman who is also Black. My gender identity is threatened simultaneously with my racial and cultural identity. And that's hard, hard.

That's why, if I'm honest, I want different for my daughter. Despite the reality, I deeply desire for her to retain her wonder, her innocence in this world for as long as possible. I want her to believe that everything is possible and that any obstacle that comes her way can be overcome. But admittedly, when you've been impacted by this kind of racial violence, it steals that from you. It's hard to see that as possible. You know that she will live in a country that's going to challenge her based on the color of her skin. You know that she'll have to shift and adapt and change the way she moves just like you did and your mother did and your grandmother did, and so on.

My sweet girl is a loving, energetic, excitable child. There are times when we are in a mall or at a store when she moves with such freedom and such confidence and, in my mind, such a lack of awareness of what the world might be perceiving of her as a young Black girl that I cringe. As I said, I know there's going to come a day when that confidence and boldness, that ability to say exactly what she wants and to express her vulnerabilities and her emotions freely might come with the ultimate cost. Neither she nor her tears will be defended like the little white girls with second- and third-wave feminist mamas would be. Nobody will come to save her. I'm not even sure I will be able to.

And I feel helpless to do anything about that. That's the real violence, right? The insidious nature of racial violence is that it is not just the devastation that comes with physical harm and death. It's also the undercurrent. The thing that happens to you slowly over time, that strips and seeps the joy, love, and peace away from your soul. And I know that's not God's design. I know that God does not want that for me, does not want that for my child. But the violence is that I don't know how to move through the world any other way.

I suppose the questions I'm always left with as I explore the impact of racial violence on me, my family, and my community are these: how do I protect and liberate at the same time? How do I help my child navigate a world that is slow to see her as I do—brilliant, creative, unique, worthy—while allowing her to follow the path her freedom takes her? I don't know exactly how to do this. I can only hope that what Jesus offers us as a model can help.

I, my daughter, my mother, my homegirl are inherently worthy, inherently deserving of protection from violence. Whether a Black woman is on welfare or on drugs or a sex worker, or whether she has a doctorate, has climbed the corporate ladder, and lives in a four-bedroom, three-bath home in the suburbs, she is worthy. It's easy to establish our value within the intersection based on proximity to whiteness or based on notions of success given to us by capitalism. But that's not it, not by a long shot. A more righteous approach might be the realization that every woman, especially those of us at these intersections, are Mary and Martha and the Samaritan woman at the well. We are all Deborah and Esther *and* Rahab and Priscilla. We all reflect the image of God. We are all loved by Christ.

Chapter 3

JUSTIFIED BY LAW

We will heal by understanding that control is a mirage, but safety is constructible.

It was a hate crime. Eyewitnesses attested to the murderer saying, "Whites don't kill whites." Gregory Bush was looking for some Black people to kill on October 24, 2018. He tried my parents' church first. Before killing my cousin and Mr. Stallard at the Kroger, Bush was recorded by external cameras trying to enter the church building and yelling the name of Dylann Roof (the white supremacist who in 2015 murdered nine Black parishioners at Mother Emanuel A.M.E. Church in Charleston, South Carolina). In my mind, Bush's statement made his intentions very clear, yet in the beginning, my family and the Stallards were told that getting this prosecuted as a hate crime was a long shot at best.

Mr. Stallard's daughter Kellie reflected on that injustice, saying,

> I was angry and disappointed in the delayed response not to call this crime what it was: a hate crime. I have to deal with hate crimes, social justice, and equity every single day and [for the police] to come to me with the wait-and-see approach did not sit well. It felt like excuses. I am an attorney and was once a public defender, so I understand the criminal process. The graciousness that was given to this white murderer

angered me, because if a Black man had run out of Kroger with a gun and had a shootout with a white man and killed a white woman, the police would have killed him in the parking lot, not arrested him.

I remember my cousin Sean, Vickie's eldest son, saying that the people who were representing our family were going to *try* to get this crime, this murder, labeled as a hate crime. Hearing this incensed me. I'd just made the assumption that it would be. I mean, we had on record that the perpetrator basically admitted that the reason he shot and killed two Black people in a grocery store in a suburb of Louisville was because they were Black. That is pretty cut and dry, right? But apparently that is not the case. It took work and more investigation to get this murder labeled a hate crime, and that speaks to the ways in which Black folks have to constantly justify our own humanity and prove that the things happening to us at the hands of white people are directly related to whites' misguided notions of superiority and racial bias. The act of having to substantiate these things over and over again is its own kind of violence.

Immediately, my thought process went to solutions. *What do we need to do to make sure that this act is properly labeled as the hate crime it was?* I had to do some digging and make some phone calls to find out what criteria the crime had to meet; not surprisingly, finding that information was hard. It felt like there was some subjectivity to it, that whether something gets labeled a hate crime or not is really dependent on whether it behooves the local and state authorities to label it that way. This was so disheartening because, again, the onus is placed on the victims to prove why this particular thing happened in a particular way. As always, I kept coming back to confusion. *Why is this so hard?* But when it comes to Black folks' pain, especially here in America, it's always hard.

All of America's institutions and systems (judicial, legal, religious, policing, education, economic), at their core, enable the kind of violence we now recognize as being connected to white supremacy and white nationalism. That's a hard pill to swallow, especially since we've been force-fed American exceptionalism since kindergarten. But it's not as much of a stretch, as much of a controversial statement, when we consider that all of these institutions and the policies were founded on white supremacist principles. My fellow gardeners might understand it better this way: One doesn't plant tomatoes and expect to harvest grapes. No, you reap what you sow, and in order to get the harvest you want, you have to dig up what you don't want and plant new seeds.

Wonder why there's so much emphasis on the racial bias that shows up in law enforcement? Why seemingly every other day there's a story about a police officer's abuse of power or use of excessive force against a Black or Brown person? We only have to look to history to see the seeds of this system we are told is supposed to protect and serve. In the internet docuseries *How American Slavery Helped Create Modern-Day Policing*, we learn that slave patrols and slave catchers were the "first form of organized police in the South" and "emerged in the colony of Carolina in the early 1700s and set the tone for policing as we know it."

> Slave patrols kept tabs on the whereabouts of the enslaved. And that meant that if Black men and women were off the plantation then the slave patrol could demand to see a slave badge noting their

occupation. Slave patrols could stop and search whomever's belongings just because.

There was some overlap with the role of slave catcher and slave patrol but together they enforced the idea that Black people were second-class citizens and that white people were the authority. In organized police departments, they enforced this hierarchy too. In South Carolina, for example, by 1857, there were dozens of officers in the Charleston Police Department whose jobs were essentially to monitor the enslaved. And, though slavery was abolished after the Civil War, the spirit of tracking and policing Black folks lived on. During the Reconstruction era, Black codes were enacted . . . and they restricted how Black folks could live their lives.[1]

David A. Harris, a law professor at the University of Pittsburgh, states, "Law enforcement often was cast in the role of enforcing Jim Crow laws and other types of laws aimed at maintaining the racial caste system and keeping Black people 'in their place.' It was aimed at maintaining the racial separation."[2] So there is absolutely a connection between Black people "running away from slavery being tracked by dogs" and the use of dogs by law enforcement to terrorize Black people, especially as documented during the civil rights era. Harris says it's "a message from history." This message is directly linked to what we now call "stop-and-frisk" and racial profiling.

But the policing system is not the only system or institution where there is clear proof of sanctioned violence against Black people. Post-Reconstruction, when Jim Crow became firmly embedded in nearly every public institution via the *Plessy v. Ferguson* ruling of 1896, the strides that Black educational institutions had made—particularly historically Black colleges and universities and the schools that fed them—were threatened. Segregation meant less funding for Black schools and less resources for Black students. After the *Brown v. Board of Education* decision in 1954, there was hope that these inequities would change, but what happened is that our educational systems found more subtle ways to widen the disparities. In many states, funds for public schools come directly from real estate taxes paid by the residents of the communities where these schools exist. Lower real estate taxes generally correlate to lower-income neighborhoods, and therefore the Black, Brown, Indigenous, and immigrant students who live in those neighborhoods still don't receive the same access to resources. Sonya Ramsey writes in "The Troubled History of American Education after the Brown Decision,"

> On May 17, 1954, when the Supreme Court ruled in the Brown case that segregation in the public schools was unequal, it caused an uproar. For southerners, this decision did not just call for the end of segregated schools, it also threatened the foundation of white supremacy, which was constructed upon destructive stereotypes of black intellectual inferiority and fears of black male sexuality. This extensive negative reaction coalesced into a strategy called "massive resistance." In May 1956, 101 congressmen issued the "Southern Manifesto" that declared, "We pledge ourselves to use all lawful means to bring about a reversal of this decision which is contrary to the Constitution and to prevent the use of force in its implementation."[3]

These are all variations on the systemic violence from which Black folks have to heal. In truth, violence has always been a tool that racist white folks have used to subjugate Black people, particularly those who have found ways to survive and thrive despite all the obstacles thrown our way. We only have to take a quick glance at the historical record to see that this is true. The formerly enslaved, recently emancipated Americans who sought to build lives for themselves and their families—whether through farming and agriculture or through the development of their own institutions (colleges, churches, organizations)—were often met with resistance, some of which came in the form of terror and violence. The numbers of Black men and women who were lynched across the South—many times to an audience of white men, women, and children—reveals only a small portion of the horror that unfortunately serves as a precursor to today's atrocities. The brutality and terror that awaited Black people who participated in the Great Migration from the South to the northern and western parts of the country also show us why laws do not necessarily reflect the fullness of Black folks' humanity nor do they hold up as any measure of justice. These very systems have wielded a more subtle but devastating violence than this country has ever seen—the knowledge of the fullness of who we are and where we come from in the first place.

It's unfortunate that the simple question "Who am I?" feels different for Black folks despite it being a common existential inquiry that most humans will ask at some point in their lives. It is, however, a legitimate query into the murky heritage that the legacy of the transatlantic slave trade has left us. This is its own kind of violence. Whereas many white folks will likely be able to trace their genealogy back as far as the seventeenth century, many Black people can barely get past the U.S. Civil War before running into the typical roadblocks of poorly kept slave records, or worse, the emotional and psychological devastation that can come with seeing our great-great-grandmothers listed as property next to the livestock inventory in the will of some old white slaveholder. Personally, I didn't realize the impact my own genealogical exploration would have on me and how triggering it would be until I had already fallen down the ancestry rabbit hole.

For the last few years, I've been searching for ways to explore my heritage and to really dig into who my people were and where they were from. I had done both the standard Ancestry.com DNA test, as well as the African Ancestry test. When the latter revealed that, at least along my maternal line, I was descended from the Yoruba people of what is now known as Nigeria, I was overjoyed. But it still felt like there was some distance between what I'd learned and what felt intimate and real. I now knew the ethnic group but had no names, no actual person to whom to connect myself. So I went back to Ancestry.com to see if I could find out some specific information. A name, a location, anything would have been great. After extensive research and reviewing a number of documents, I was finally able to trace my heritage back to the 1830s and my great-great-great-grandmother, a woman apparently held on a plantation near Wilmington, North Carolina. Seeing her name, seeing words like "servant" and "slave" next to her name and the names of her children, really did something to me.

It's not because I wasn't aware this would be the outcome. I'd seen it happen many, many times before, whether with other friends doing genealogical research or on television. But I think it was the knowledge that this particular woman was connected to me. Something about making that direct linkage to yourself as opposed to it happening to someone else renders the experience very different. Doing that work started me really thinking about all of the women in my family line. What were their stories? What traumas did they carry? What joys did they hold in their bodies? Their arrival onto these shores had to be marked with pain, but then how did they learn to make a life—in North Carolina, Virginia, New York, Kentucky, and all the other places they laid down roots? I don't know; I was just really moved by it. I was also very sad. These were stories I'd never know.

And as I said before, *not knowing* is itself a kind of violence, especially when I know that the reason I don't know is because my third-great-grandmother and second-great-grandmother were treated the same as cattle. My great-grandmother and grandmother, and yes, even my mother, born the year that *Brown v. Board of Education* finally outlawed segregation, were all also seen as inferior. The hard truth is that, for most Black folks in America, centuries of our heritage were stolen from us, and that disconnect lives deeply in our bodies and our psyches even if we are unaware of it.

Is it a reach to characterize as violence the lack of access to our genealogical stories because of actual dehumanizing laws? It is not. Most people understand the value of knowing your roots. Even the biblical record reflects that importance. Those parts of the Bible that often cause us to sigh in exhaustion—John begat Joe who begat Tony—are prevalent in numerous passages of Scripture (see Gen. 4; Ruth 4; Matt. 1). And there are reasons why the Hebrew and Greek and Aramaic texts take us on those journeys. There's value in knowing our lineage. And when that lineage has been cut off, damage is done.

Even within the last one hundred years, as part of the Great Migration, the evidence of Black folks attempting to either reclaim our heritage or create new narratives about our journey here is clear. As much as the Great Migration was about leaving the terror of the South, it was also about the establishment of a future that acknowledged the past but didn't live in the same spaces as the hard parts of that history. On the other side of my family, my research shows that, at some point, we were enslaved in Alabama. Members of our family, mostly women, found their way north to Kentucky and west to Texas. And while it's a shame that I don't know their names and don't have a record of their stories, I still believe that there's something powerful about taking up your bags and searching for freedom, even when nothing indicates that freedom can be found. It's a healing act, I think. Taking nothing away from those who stayed— because it's also a healing act to stand and be courageous and not be moved—I see leaving as grasping for healing in the face of violence big and small, and it's good to know that this too was something that was passed down to me.

But what can't be denied is that the Great Migration didn't happen in a vacuum. These beautiful people were leaving the only places they'd ever known for a reason: racial violence. Nearly four thousand Black men were being hung for minor reasons or no reason at all by both terrorist groups like the KKK and "good" white folks alike. We can't ignore that. If I'm going to write a book about racial violence, I cannot ignore all the iterations of how that violence has shown up, particularly in this country, in order to make Christian white folks feel comfortable. If I have to read those census records and cry painful tears at my third-great-grandmother's untold story, then white folks need to be willing to stare into the eyes of those people in the photos of lynching "events" where white people who look like them are smiling with their children and selling body parts as souvenirs. As I stare into the void of my heritage, I call white people to stare into the reality of theirs. Maybe this is the starting point of understanding the impact of the history of racial violence in this country. Maybe then, the recent fight to erase this well-documented history—a fight led by many white people who identify as Christians—will be seen as the violence it is.

It's enough that Black scholars have had to fight to have these stories told, but to pretend as though this terror didn't exist at all does nothing to heal the rift the violence caused in the first place. In the college-level African American literature course I teach, taken by both Black and white students, I use a Critical Race Theory lens as a way to discuss and offer a contextual and cultural understanding of the texts we are reading. I know from experience that helping students understand what real life looked like—the good, bad, and ugly—for Black people living in the early twentieth century, what the racial climate was during that time period, is critical to increasing their engagement with Alice Walker's novel *The Color Purple* or Zora Neale Hurston's novel *Their Eyes Were Watching God* or August Wilson's play *Joe Turner's Come and Gone*. That engagement, for many of my white students, inspires understanding and in some cases empathy. Taking the potential of that empathy away from my Black and Brown students is a kind of violence all its own, especially since there is also so much present-day residue to handle.

   Kidada Williams, author of *They Left Great Marks on Me: African American Testimonies of Racial Violence from Emancipation to World War I*, attests to this very thing as she recounts the stories of newly freed Black people who courageously spoke about their experiences with racial violence before an 1871 congressional committee as well as in other print publications:

> This near silence in the scholarly literature on African Americans' specific representations of the impact of violence on them is unfortunate because blacks who testified about their experiences of racial violence were an exceptional class of people who had to overcome great odds to have their testimonies entered into the public record. These women, men, and children endured and witnessed some of the most violent desecrations of the social compact established by Reconstruction: that blacks and whites would coexist without slavery. They are exceptional because these people surmounted many victims' instinctive desires to banish memories of horrible events, which for black people in the postemancipation South ranged from the daily attacks on their bodies, psyches, and homes to the terrors of nightriding, lynching, massacring, and rioting. Regardless of the form violence took, it was a weapon that white Americans used to deny African Americans the opportunity to enjoy their citizenship rights. Violent whites achieved some success in their efforts to subjugate African Americans. Like survivors of other human atrocities, some black people subjected to racial violence were too traumatized and therefore psychologically incapable of bearing witness to what happened to them and relating it to others. In fact, scholarship on trauma suggests that even those who were able to relive traumatic events often did not want to relate

their experiences to others for fear that they would be attacked or that listeners would not believe them.[4]

A great deal of the pushback and resistance to social justice actions seems to be based in this strange emphasis on laws over human life, under the guise of having respect for the allegedly just laws of the land. I find that many white Christians like to use obedience to the law as a way to not deal with the ways in which those same laws are unjust. Saying to a Black person or to a marginalized group, "Well, if you just obey the law, if you just don't block streets, if you just don't resist arrest, if you just don't do these things, then that would make it better for you," doesn't allow for all the past laws that have been found to be unjust. Until 1863 in this country, enslaving another human was legal. Jim Crow and the laws that put forth separate but equal via *Plessy v. Ferguson* were the law of the land until someone stood up and said, "These laws are unjust."

Even when talking about the economic violence that Black and Brown folks experience, many people say, "Oh, well, taxes are what they are." They quote Mark 12:17, where Jesus says to render to Caesar what belongs to Caesar, and to give to God what belongs to God. But what they fail to see are the intentions of the Pharisees, which ironically aren't far off from the disingenuous intentions of those who throw around these Scripture verses. Jesus understands that the Pharisees are trying to trap him. They are trying to use the law as a way to arrest Jesus, to say why his work and his ministry are not valid and are in opposition to what they claim to believe. Sound familiar? This isn't very different from the ways in which many people use the law as a way to say that people who are standing up for their rights and demanding justice are somehow wrong for doing so. It's a complete misreading of the text.

The civil disobedience that occurs is a result of unjust laws and a demand for people to see God in marginalized groups. To render unto God what is God's includes the humans that reflect the image of God.

Well, Tracey, unjust laws are a thing of the past. People today are more open-minded!

I wish it were just a process of waiting for all the "bad white folks" to die off. Unfortunately, the racial violence that history reveals to us is directly linked to what we still see today. Yes, as noted, the mid-twentieth century brought masses of Black people to the North and West in order to escape some of the extreme forms of violence experienced in the South and with the hopes of a better life. But what is often missed in these conversations on the resilience of Black folks during this time is the fact that trauma travels just as well as racism does. The biases of white folks in the North manifested as shutting Black workers out of unions and redlining communities to keep successful Black people from integrating white neighborhoods. Again, this is its own kind of violence.

But didn't we have a civil rights movement that fixed all of that? Before that time, of course, there were some issues.

After the Civil Rights Act of 1964 and the assassination of Rev. Dr. Martin Luther King Jr. in 1968, President Richard Nixon instituted a "war on drugs" that we now know was part of the racist southern strategy that flipped the Republican Party from the party of Lincoln to something entirely different. In fact, it was well into the 1990s before policies and laws even remotely began to line up with principles of equity. But even now, poverty and mass incarceration, and wage and wealth gaps abound during a time when individualism and capitalism are flaunted as the only way out. I would venture to say that the overwhelm created by these disparities opens the door for hopelessness within Black communities to seep into our story.

When I have hope, something happens in my body. A tingle in my chest feels like anticipation. And no matter what's going on around me, if I can feel that tingle, if I can sense in my fingertips this kind of positive anxiety, this kind of forward movement, I know that hope is present. And even if I'm standing still, if I can grasp hope even in the most desperate of ways, then I will hold onto it no matter what. But racial violence steals that feeling. It replaces that feeling in our bodies with something else, so what was once hope, propelling us to our destiny, propelling us to what-ever the next step in our lives happens to be, is replaced with a kind of dread—and so that anticipation of something good turns into a hopelessness or an anticipation of some-thing bad.

As writer and scholar Imani Perry wrote in a *New York Times* profile of legendary and elusive Black writer Gayl Jones, "The terror of now is as important a sub-ject for the Black imagination as a speculatively beautiful tomorrow."[5] That resonates.

This is at the core of what we understand about post-traumatic stress disorder (PTSD). When hopelessness, despair, or any other trigger causes my heart to race, my breathing to speed up, and my brain to spin, I know my body is reacting in such a way, however distorted, to keep me safe—because it believes that there is a threat. Whether that threat is actual doesn't matter. If a trigger says, "This is very much like that thing that happened back then," then our body will choose safety every time. There is no moving forward. There is no assumption of treatment that doesn't include violence in whatever form. This disruption has a buffet of ailments to choose from when it decides to show up. Panic attack and disease on one end of the spectrum, drugs, alcohol, sex, and everything in between—all because the body's goal is to try to stop what has happened before, or the potential of something like what happened before, from happening again.

My cousin Marcus Jones, Vickie's youngest son, says,

I still see a therapist and am constantly reminded of that day. I live by the Kroger and pass it daily, but I can't go close to it. At times, I am especially reminded when hearing about other shootings around the United States. I'm working on healing, and I know it's a long process. I was still angry [during the trial]. I was numb. [White people] only recognize this issue when it hits close to home, but any other time it's not their concern. This is something Black people have to deal with daily.

Marcus's brother Sean echoes those feelings:

Initially, it felt like a bad dream. I kept telling myself that there was no way someone shot my innocent mother who wouldn't hurt anyone. Then disbelief quickly turned to anger. The anger caused me to distance myself from everyone, for fear of not knowing how I would react to anything. My body was constantly tense, back spasming. I immediately sought out mental help.

My mind has not been the same since. I have a psychologist and have been in therapy since it happened. During the trial, I was an emotional roller coaster. I constantly thought of ways to get past the law enforcement officers that were guarding [the shooter]. I thought of many different ways to take him out. Through prayer and hearing my mother's voice in my head, I didn't. I could hear her saying, "He is just sick, don't hurt him."

One of the devastating consequences of racial violence, especially when it hits close to home, is that it creates a sense that you aren't safe no matter what. That lack of safety creates a sense of despair and hopelessness that disrupts any possibility of those tingles showing up. Trauma disrupts joy. Accessing peace is disrupted by the wounding. Bodily liberation is disrupted by this thing that has told us that, no matter what, we are in danger. I experienced this intensely right after my cousin's murder, when simply going into a grocery store would send me to a terrifying place. I would locate all the exits and peek down aisles before going into them. I had constant feelings of terror in my body that may not have made sense to anyone else, but did to me because my body understood that if this woman whom I loved and admired could go into this place and randomly be killed, then I could too. If it was possible that my skin color could make me a target, particularly in environments that are predominately white, then it was impossible to feel safe. My body decided to act *as if*. This thing—being murdered—was now in the realm of possibility, so it made sense for my body to respond as if it were actually happening. And how did I respond? I did not go into grocery stores or any large building with bright lights and wide-open spaces. Freedom of movement was no longer a possibility. There was limit on my liberation.

Kellie Stallard Watson felt that even her freedom to breathe was limited.

At this time in 2018, I was going through breast reconstruction from breast cancer. The week before this, I had surgery as part of that reconstruction. My chest was hurting and felt tight. I realized that I was holding my breath a lot, and often had to remind myself to breathe. I was getting questions from every-one, about everything, and I remember thinking that I wanted to scream for people to leave me alone. I kept looking at my phone, thinking that my dad was going to text or call. I was worried and scared for my son. I didn't want him to leave my sight. This pain I felt, I had never felt anything like that. I was wor-ried and scared for my mother and my brother, for my niece and nephews. I also felt guilty. My dad was helping me. He was picking my son up from school and taking him to get supplies for a project so that I would not have to do it. I was also angry. Very angry. I had a lot to do and decisions to make, so I really did not allow myself to address how I was feeling because there was so much to do.

For me, even after being in therapy for years prior to 2018, I still didn't realize that my avoidance of these places was actually a response to that trauma. I tried to put all kinds of other names on it, to call it something else. *Maybe my eyes are not adjusting well to the bright lights of these big-box stores.* My eyes were fine. My body just knew some-thing I didn't. It knew that whether it was a resistance to conversations about implicit bias training or creating stron-ger gun laws or immigration reform, many of the laws and lawmakers of this country had created an environment that has emboldened the worst of white folks, as writer Kiese Laymon would call them, and they could kill me with impunity. Not to mention that even getting these crimes legally named properly is beyond hard.

There's a case to be made for maintaining hope, for pursuing both personal and global healing. The way we heal from hopelessness is to send it back to its source. Like a piece of mail delivered to us but not addressed to us, we "return to sender," if you will. I can decide that my joy can't be stolen, even if it's temporarily paused. Sure, my sorrow and rage, my pain, say to burn it all down. It says that any white person who would dare excuse or rationalize or erase the racial violence that my ancestors and I have endured doesn't deserve my time nor energy; they certainly don't deserve my compassion. And I would be 100 percent right. However, the way healing works, the way true change and transformation happen, is when we leave room for the possibility that there is fertile soil underneath all that scorched earth.

I've spent the last decade unraveling myself from some of the faith traditions of my childhood and rebuilding a life rooted in spiritual intimacy with God through the particular incarnation of Jesus. Like everyone else, I also spent nearly two years as of this writing navigating a global pandemic—from quarantine to a return to socially distanced activities and back again. There is no question that the depth of the work required for the former has supported my ability to do the latter.

I know that the prevailing argument, particularly in hard-to-see-the-horizon days like these, is that religion in general is the opiate of the masses. Even as a believer, I

accept this as true—mostly because the notions of unconditional love and eternal rest are wonderfully addictive concepts when faced in a crisis with the lack of the former and
the pernicious threat of the latter. Yet I also know that our
faith can be the driver of our liberation—Black and white—
if we are willing to take our hands off the wheel and remove
the veils from our eyes. If white people who love God would
be willing to de-center themselves in every space where
there is an assumption of supremacy or entitlement and do
the hard work of listening to the lived experience of Black
folks with a heart toward empathy as opposed to salvation,
that would be a start. Nothing will be definite. There is no
guarantee of being liked or loved or understood. The only
goal is healing.

Lots of things were lost in my so-called deconstruction. Specifically demolished were the places where
patriarchal and white supremacist ideologies masked as theologies. Yet my biggest loss—certainty—has actually been
my greatest stabilizer. Lack of certainty has forced me into
the proverbial arms of God, where I've felt safer than I ever
did memorizing and reciting Scripture verses or attempting
to be good for goodness' sake. At one time I desperately
wanted to believe in the absolutes the church taught me.
Even within the Black church, this notion of respectability
as the ticket to escaping the worst of white supremacy was
enticing. If one lived this way—say, as a kind and generous person—then the outcome should be that they would
never experience any trials. If one thought positively, then
the reactions received would always be positive. While
the Golden Rule, Karma, and even Newton's third law of
motion all validate this to some degree, I also know that
none of these principles, nor respectability, and certainly
not the admonitions to walk the straight and narrow put

forth by the church mean that awful things won't happen, that good people won't die, that racism will not continue to rear its ugly head whenever and however it sees fit—even in the midst of a pandemic.

COVID-19 illuminated for me the very nature of faith as the belief in something one cannot see, the hope for something one cannot fathom. It's the only safety available to me. In this case, losing my attachment to certainty— whether talking about racism or the pandemic or racism *within* the pandemic—gives me perspective. I can hope for a miracle in the face of death, or I can work toward a shift in policy that will maybe, hopefully, force a shift in mindset. I can believe that something is on the other side of isolation, even when I don't know when that other side is coming. In this way, there is great significance in having a faith tradition to grasp when everything else is shifting.

And for Black folks, it's always shifting. For many of us, faith is a literal safe place when violence and death are all around. In the words of the Psalmist,

> Whoever dwells in the shelter of the Most High
>   will rest in the shadow of the Almighty.
> I will say of the LORD, "He is my refuge and my fortress,
>   my God, in whom I trust."
>
> Surely he will save you
>   from the fowler's snare
>   and from the deadly pestilence.
> He will cover you with his feathers,
>   and under his wings you will find refuge;
>   his faithfulness will be your shield and rampart.
> You will not fear the terror of night,
>   nor the arrow that flies by day,

nor the pestilence that stalks in the darkness,
   nor the plague that destroys at midday.
A thousand may fall at your side,
   ten thousand at your right hand,
   but it will not come near you.

                             Ps. 91:1–7 NIV

To be clear—and maybe this is a place where some wrestling might need to happen—when I speak of faith as a safe place, as a place where healing from racial violence can begin for us all, I'm not talking about religious systems, mostly fundamentalist—and in the case of Christianity, usually evangelical—that use political and faulty theological scaffolding to remake the face of Jesus, the Prophets, Muhammad, Buddha, and the like into homogenized versions of white male dominance. There's actually very little authentic faith present there. By "authentic faith," I mean the spiritual relationships and encounters, the principles and tenets that inform our morality and drive our desire to love and serve humanity the best we know how. The belief that one can be a vessel for the demonstration of God's love in the face of either human destruction or nature's disruption is one of the many ways faith can be valuable in this healing process.

The concept of faith itself, with all its nuances, is hard for nonbelievers to wrap their minds around during good times, and yet it's generally the very thing people cling to in a crisis. This is primarily because most of us—even believers—resist the accountability that faith and faith traditions require and maybe, more specifically, how our frail humanity chooses to enact that accountability. We hate what we perceive as rules unless we come up with them and they serve our own perceived entitlements. I would even submit that there is a through line between the rules created by the institutional church as a way to maintain control and power and the unjust laws in the world beyond its walls, also created to maintain control and power.

Much of our resistance is less about the existence of God or the inability to reconcile the theology of any particular sacred text and more about our feelings of inadequacy in meeting what we believe are the hard-and-fast rules found in those texts. I was taught way back during my childhood Sunday school classes that the B.I.B.L.E. was my Basic Instructions Before Leaving Earth. I would later learn that these "instructions" were anything but basic. We are hard-pressed to embrace grace for ourselves and others—until, of course, we are faced with scenarios that require it in order for us to survive, those situations where nothing makes sense. That constriction in our movements forces us to look for spiritual guides because our natural ones have failed us.

Black folks live right there.

And even those who vehemently question why we hold on to the notion of Jesus' salvation so tightly, who wrongly dismiss the faith because of how it was wielded by barbarians during the transatlantic slave trade and the colonization of Black and Brown lands by those driven by greed, white supremacy, and spiritual vacuity, can recognize the powerful lure of grace. Faith functions as a place of grounding in the face of crisis and trauma. Even if it doesn't serve any other purpose, I would say that this is a worthy one.

If for no other reason, faith is a useful tool for healing from racial trauma because the inexplicable joy that comes with the hope of a better—yes, even eternal—tomorrow releases the hormones necessary to strengthen the immune system and reduce the stress hormones (cortisol and the like) that can send Black bodies into arrest.

Some would argue that's a stretch, yet I submit that if we can embrace the firmly supported notion that God created a connection between our minds and our bodies (biology shows us that the way we think impacts how our body responds), then the leap to there being a connection between our mind, body, and spirit only requires that we release our hold on certainty and accept a spiritual reality that lives simultaneously outside and within of us. This is how Black folks will heal. This is also how white people will heal.

Having faith, in whatever degree, opens up the possibility of miracles, of both individual change and collective transformation, of that police officer being finally held accountable for murdering an unarmed Black man, of that woman who called the police on children playing in a park being held accountable by her own neighbors, of the white people watching it all actually feeling the weight of these injustices and taking steps to change the system—or, yes, burning it all down if necessary.

For me and many Black people, holding on to faith makes us willing to see another day when we otherwise would give up. It presses us to create rituals that help sustain us in a near-meditation on hope. We, out of necessity, transfer our hope from failed governments and political leaders to something we hope is greater, and whether that hope is warranted or not, it is the thing that helps us keep on living, as our elders would say.

Faith has taught me that it is impossible to dismantle broken systems without broken hearts being healed. Broken little white boys become broken white men, and broken white men placed in a system that prioritizes money, white supremacy, patriarchy, and capitalism over human lives and dignity means that you have leadership such as what we have experienced recently. Because authentic faith across all religious traditions prioritizes the marginalized and poor, faith is the great leveler. It tears down the monuments we've made of men and focuses on what's important—a national, if not global, community in need of healing. That said, faith is also a fearless healer. It helps us be unafraid to confront that kind of leadership because it affirms the belief that we don't answer to any human. Faith both humbles and strengthens us under a divine sovereignty. Simultaneously, it infuses us with hope—a kind of supernatural alchemy—that ultimately transforms our grief and sorrow into the strength necessary to stand firm in the face of a system that justifies racial violence and the trauma that follows. Challenging these systems is absolutely an act of faith. It is a belief that our actions matter even when the certainty we so desperately desire escapes us.

On the other hand, sometimes those of us who are grieving as a result of racial violence cannot bring ourselves to think about challenging systems when our hearts are so broken, even when we know we must. There's a kind of pain that blurs our vision and mutes our ears to anything that takes the focus off our loved one's life. Even more aggravating is the inevitable conversation that comes up when we talk about our loss, about the alleged sovereignty of God. Even as I consider what it means to heal in the context of my faith, I can't help but hear the words of well-meaning family, friends, and churchgoers: words that make me cringe on the inside, even as I smile on the outside; well-intentioned but incensing words delivered by those who desire to comfort the grieving:

"Maybe it was just your cousin's time."

"You loved her, but God loved her best."

"God will deliver us in his own time."

That's hard. Real hard. I suppose I'd say what I tell my ten-year-old when she asks the hard questions. It's what every person of faith has to be willing to say if we want to heal: I don't know. The truth is, the very nature of a higher power necessitates a belief in the mystery of that higher power. A God I understand is not a God worthy of my worship. What I do know is that believing that the earthly realm is only one stop on a longer journey of the soul is a salve for my broken heart. I don't get mad at God when a family member moves to the other side of the earth, so I refuse to get mad at God because a family member moves on to another dimension, no matter how unjust that move is. I can be sad. My sorrow might even overwhelm me as the tsunami of grief often does. But my faith is the thing that steadies me—and in a time when death and sickness lurk around every corner, when Black mothers and partners worry about our sons and husbands every time we send them out the door—a faith that steadies is a faith that can heal.

The justifications that many make about our laws—this idea that laws are never to be questioned—neglects the fact that laws are made by people, and most of the time, those people have a particular agenda. At the core of all of it is the need for control and the desire for certainty.

Stripping away, at the soul level, the notion that whiteness is somehow greater than, better than, or the standard by which all other groups should follow leaves many white people with a sense of uncertainty, maybe even a

crisis of identity. This might explain why, behind the political and social grab for power, there is this belief that one
can legislate one's own or another's being. Can any of us
truly legislate our places in the world? Maybe not. But the
attempts to embed in our systems whiteness as a standard,
and anything not identifiably white as inferior, seem to be
an attempt to do that very thing. So part of our healing is
really understanding that what we are trying to control is
not real, and the certainty we're grasping for is really just
another construct.

The need for control and certainty provides the perfect climate for violence because it assumes that there's a
legitimate threat. The only threat white people really face
is to the status quo they've built to maintain an advantage
based on one's skin color. If you're operating in such a way
that you believe Black and Brown folks are a real threat,
then you're absolutely going to try to legislate ways to keep
you and yours safe—and you'll also be willing to uphold, or
at the very least overlook, violence to do that. And historically, the way white people have enacted that control has
always been violent. We've seen it for at least a millennium,
if not more. That need for control and, dare I say, domination is one major factor that leads to the false notions and
stereotypes that are the foundations of white supremacy.
Colonization, this idea of conquering a country or community, taking ownership of it, is just one example of control
implemented by violence, but there are others. The healing
work is about getting to the root of this skewed perspective
and uprooting these stereotypes about Black and Brown
folks from the start.

It's important to realize that in order for us to really
heal from the trauma that's created by racial violence, we

must be willing to surrender our need for control. White folks who claim Christ as savior must be willing to reckon with how much damage to their own souls and to their own notions of salvation the desire for certainty has caused. Weaponizing certainty is enacted in many ways—whether through a vote or financial support. What damage does this desire to maintain the status quo do to your own soul and to those who are marginalized by your actions?

Chapter 4
SILENCE IS VIOLENCE
We will heal when we are better stewards
of this life in every way.

I could feel the anticipation throbbing in my bones. It's not like we had never gone to church before. Of course, we'd gone every Sunday. But this felt different. I needed to hear something from the pastor that I wasn't quite sure I was going to hear. After spending many years in predominantly Black churches, my husband and I decided to begin attending a multicultural, nondenominational church. The pastor is biracial, but many of the people in leadership are white—and I had deep concerns in that moment because I'd just watched a man be killed in front of his daughter and fiancé on a video clip that had, by then, traveled around the world. I needed my church to understand why that experience and the experiences I'd been having over the last few years had shaken me to my core.

I suppose I needed there to be some acknowledgment of my pain, some addressing of how I might navigate it. I needed my church to get off the fence, to no longer play the "We don't see color, race is not an issue here, we are a utopia" card, and actually see *me* for a change—to see what my culture, what Black folks have been dealing with, and be willing to stand in the gap, if necessary, for me in the same ways they stand in the gap for all the other horrifying challenges people face.

There was never a question that when sex trafficking had become a problem in our city, my church would be involved in advocating for the women and children who had been taken into these rings. When the issue of homelessness intensified, the church had no problem with providing services and comfort to those who were unhoused. We even had small groups that were dedicated to particular issues, some addressing the challenges of divorce or terminal illness. Yet up until that point, I'd seen no effort to deal with or even simply talk about the horrors of racial violence and racism that I knew Black and Brown folks in our congregation were wrestling with, and no effort to comfort them.

So on this particular Sunday, not long after the murder of Philando Castile, I was hoping for something different. I was hoping I would walk into the church service and hear my pastor be unequivocal about the church's position against racial violence, discrimination, white supremacy, and implicit bias. That was my prayer. But my bones knew my hopes were too high. My body tried to warn me. There's that funny thing called hope again. Black folks keep showing up, keep hoping that things will be different because it's the only way to survive and, in some cases, to outright live.

We walked into the service, and after dropping our daughter off at children's church, we sat down. It's one of those contemporary services where you can bring your coffee in, so I had my coffee, and my husband and I kept stealing glances at each other throughout the service. The praise team sang the first song, and then sang the second. Then the pastor got up to speak. When he opened with, "There's a lot of hard things happening in our world today," my heart leaped in my chest. *Yeah, there is.* And then he went on to read an unrelated passage of Scripture and preach a sermon on a topic I can no longer remember because it was 100 percent *not* about racial violence, trauma, or any related matter. Afterward, the praise team sang another song and service was over. I was numb. "Yes, Pastor," I wanted to scream. "There *are* a lot of hard things happening in our world. And one of the hardest things is that our churches are unwilling to disrupt the status quo by addressing what is a real and present issue for a large segment of the body of Christ in this country!" But I did not scream that. I picked up my empty coffee cup, followed my husband to the children's church room, and went home.

It's not the white-supremacy-fueled resistances from white Christians who actively stand against anything that even remotely looks like racial reckoning that hurts the most for many Black Christians. Sadly, that's expected. It's the collective inaction of so-called woke white people within the body of Christ that burns us the most. I wonder if the use of "Black body" as a placeholder for "Black people" has created a kind of disconnect for those who claim to be allies. I've used the term frequently in my work because it speaks to the somatic nature of trauma. But I also know that white folks, in general, don't see Black bodies as worthy and valuable. And "good" white church folks, often in an effort to counter racism, intentionally ignore or disregard Black bodies in an effort to "not see color." So I wonder if the silence that is wielded is the result of a deep-rooted indifference toward Black bodies. And maybe if one can connect that body to a soul, a spirit, then the stakes will seem high enough for their voices to be lifted in outrage. Maybe the discomfort one feels in having to center someone else's lived experience will lessen when one realizes that those experiences are not happening in a vacuum. That these acts of violence, physical or psychological, are happening to actual people whom God loves. While we certainly can and must talk about the killing of Black bodies, we cannot forget the slaying of Black spirits by the very institutions in which we're supposed to find solace.

One of the things that has taken me over forty years to really wrap my mind around when it comes to my own childhood trauma (I am a survivor of sexual abuse and sexual assault) is just how much of my PTSD response comes not from the actual things that happened to me but from the silence that followed. The truth is, when things finally settled down after my childhood abuse, the one thing that disturbed my adolescent self was the fact that nobody talked about it. Nobody talked to *me* about it. Nobody allowed me to talk about it. It was something that happened, a secret, and once it was allegedly resolved, I was supposed to put it away somewhere. The problem was, nobody told me where to put it. So I hid it in my body, and years later, when the mysterious aches and pains showed up, I'd forgotten that I'd put it there.

I was immersed in silence, and I think more than anything, this did more damage to me than even the actual abuse because I truly had no place to put my pain. Unfortunately, within the Black community in the 1980s, and especially in the church, therapy was something white people did. It had a stigma associated with it. Where I came from, you prayed, asked God to help you, and you survive. That's it. Therapy was almost seen as a demonstration of a lack of faith. I'm grateful that I've since learned that that's so far from the truth. I'm sad that it took me nearly forty years.

Even as a child, there were things I needed to know, things I needed to understand about why this thing had happened and why it wasn't my fault. I needed someone to teach me how to move through the world without this shame that had deeply embedded itself in my mind, body, and soul. I wanted to be free, but I didn't know how to release it all. And as I said, nobody ever talked about it. There was so much silence around what happened to me that I internalized that silence as evidence that I lacked value, that I wasn't worthy of protection, love, or healing. As a result, I spent my early twenties turning those feelings of rejection into behavior that did not serve me well. I sought love and relationships from people who honestly were representative of what I'd always known. They were emotionally disconnected, unavailable.

When I think about my personal experience, I can't help but consider the impact of silence on the collective of Black folks. I can see how, above and beyond the actual events of racial violence—say, the eight minutes and forty-six seconds that Derek Chauvin held his knee on George Floyd's neck, the numerous not-guilty verdicts—what aggravates many Black people is the fact that those injustices are followed by a stark silence, particularly from the church. It feels like white Christians believe that if we don't talk about race—the "r-word"—then they don't have to confront it. The pain that racial violence causes goes unseen and ignored. Too many Black folks are sitting in churches, just like I was, waiting for someone to see them, hear them, love them, stand in solidarity with them. We are sitting there hoping that the teachings on "Bear one another's burdens" (Gal. 6:2) and "Weep with those who weep" (Rom. 12:15) are true. And sometimes we are seeking a way rooted in love that will allow the rage to not consume us.

But nobody wants to talk about it. Nobody wants to call out just how far from God's will these events are and stand on that. Maybe because challenging the wrongness of

racism and racial violence means having to interrogate what
one has believed about Black people and the biases that
have been held. Maybe because standing in solidarity with
me means sitting with all the ways one has, even indirectly,
benefited from a system that is responsible for my pain and
the death of so many. Not having the courage to contend
with all of this could definitely be one reason why silence,
despite the complicity attached to it, seems to be the safe
and preferable response.

Wrestling with the harm caused by silence and wanting change requires being amenable to being called out or
called in without resistance—to accept that even one's unintentional actions can cause harm, that one's inability to see
what Black people might be going through translates into a
disregard for our lived experiences and possibly a centering
of one's own. There have been so many instances when,
whether out of frustration, anger, or exhaustion, Black folks
have very directly and distinctly called white folks out on
overtly racist action or even seemingly minor microaggressions and instead of sitting with it and allowing God to use
it to heal one's blind spots, the person becomes defensive.
This defensiveness is in itself a violent act and creates a bar-
rier to what this person can learn from the experience. As
Toni Morrison said in her Nobel Prize lecture, "Oppressive language does more than represent violence; it is violence; does more than represent the limits of knowledge; it
limits knowledge."[1]

I've observed even the most progressive allies balk
at the idea that they're being called out and attempt to shift
the focus from the harmful action to the way that it's being
called out. Now instead of having a conversation about the
power of one's actual words or actions, we are mired in an

unfruitful form of tone policing that essentially boils down to a white person saying, "You have to be nicer to me in order to get me to do what I already know I need to do"— as if this notion of niceness is somehow going to make the person more willing to listen to being called out.

This defensiveness is actually another way to be in control and dominate Black and Brown folks, even within the context of allyship. And it leaves no opportunity for unjust laws to change or for healing to happen.

That said, it's also likely that the silence of white Christians and the church in general is the result of an inability to make the connections between all the events of history that have been named as violent or reflective of white supremacy. The ability to connect the dots between colonization, the transatlantic slave trade, Jim Crow, the twenty-first-century uprisings, and what happened to my cousin is critical.

There's absolutely a link between George Floyd in Minneapolis and Breonna Taylor in Louisville and the Charleston Nine and Dajerria Becton in McKinney, Texas, and Freddie Gray in Baltimore and Michael Brown in Ferguson and Tamir Rice in Cleveland and Eric Garner in Staten Island and Trayvon Martin in Sanford, Florida, and, and, and. . . . This link is a thread that is both old and strong. It's the same thread that linked Amadou Diallo and James Byrd and Emmett Till and the burning of Black Wall Street and the lynchings of Black men and women in the South. And the first knot in that thread—threading of the needle, if you will—happened along the Middle Passage. While the thread certainly shapeshifts, it has never been cut off, as it has proven quite lucrative over the last four hundred years.

Think my thread metaphor is too generous? Artistic theologian Alexus Rhone pulled no punches in her assessment when I spoke with her about this: "You call it a 'thread,' Tracey, but I call it a demonic spirit imbued within the fabric of a nation too proud to bend in humility and mourn the sins of their fathers that have literally been passed down to their children. Instead of exorcising the demons, they've signed peace treaties with them."[2]

To be clear, the thread I'm talking about, the demonic spirit Alexus is referencing, is white supremacy. And the manifestation of its presence is exactly what we are seeing today: the evidence that Black lives really don't matter. I recognize that our instinct is to compartmentalize these conversations, to say that the church is different. It is not.

Antagonism aside, the deafening silence of the body of Christ as a collective on the recent injustices against people of color here in the United States and around the world is evidence to me of the insidious, cancerous infiltration of racism and white supremacy in *our* body. It is harmful and deadly.

> That he might present it to himself a glorious church, not having spot, or wrinkle, or any such thing; but that it should be holy and without blemish. (Eph. 5:27 KJV)

Jesus isn't as interested in perfect individuals as the church is. I do believe that he is interested in a church that is unified in its awareness of its blood-washed sins and has accomplished his mission with all the grace he did on earth. He's interested in a church that has, at a very basic level, maintained the two greatest commandments: to love God and to love our neighbors as ourselves (Matt. 22:37–39). Unfortunately, because the institution of the church is just as divided as this country, we remain as spotted, wrinkled, and blemished as anything else.

It is deeply affecting our witness to the world.

If the body of Christ stood unified and willing to fight this evil—not on the basis that we agree on every political or social issue, but on the basis that we follow the same Jesus who died on the cross for every single one of us and commanded that we stand up for those who are considered the "least"—what message would that send to the world? What an amazing act of love that would be.

Ironically, some white folks right now, heading to their local Black Lives Matter protest or prayer vigil or donating to the next hashtagged person's family's GoFundMe page, still find themselves anxious when I use the phrase "white supremacy." They are ready to put this book down or vent to their friends about all the reasons why they're so tired of people like me "playing the race card" because "everything isn't about race" or ignoring the entitlement in saying, "What more do you want? Why alienate good people who want to help?"

One point is right. Everything isn't about race. But some things are. Given the history of our country, many things are. And on those many things, I tend to play the cards how they're dealt. White supremacy conjures up images of skinheads and men in white robes rather than corporate boardrooms, city halls, and black robes. Shifting the language means that a rather neutral or even progressive white person might have to recognize their wonderful papa or sweet nana as a white supremacist. Embracing this is hard—and also a necessary part of the healing process.

RobtheIdealist did a great job of speaking to the impact of white supremacy in his post on the now-defunct web magazine *Orchestrated Pulse*:

> We so often want to speak in terms of who *is* and isn't racist, thus treating racism as an individual state of being, rather than a system of power. Racism is not merely a personal attitude or an insult; instead, it's a racial system of power maintained by violence (with the violence often going unpunished because it is protected by the dominant system of power). Therefore, an individual can be perpetuating this system without even being conscious of their actions.
>
> Ultimately, we are all complicit in the perpetuation of systemic white supremacy, but we are not all equally culpable, nor do we all benefit equally. We must make sure that the discussion is multidimensional.

Consider this: if you find yourself sitting in your home and hearing about nine Black people in a church Bible study being killed in Charleston because of a murderous terrorist's false belief that Black people are somehow "taking over the country," and your first instinct is to find a justification *other* than racism—you don't shed one tear, your spirit doesn't rage with a desire for justice, you don't see the blatant disparities in how this suspect was treated as opposed to any of the Black men and women who encounter police, you don't even bow your head in prayer to ask God to send his Holy Spirit to comfort those who have lost their loved ones—then you might want to consider how deeply rooted white supremacy is in your own bloodline. Because this:

Rejoice with those who rejoice, weep with those who weep. (Rom. 12:15)

And this:

Blessed be the God and Father of our Lord Jesus Christ, the Father of mercies and God of all consolation, who consoles us in all our affliction, so that we may be able to console those who are in any affliction with the consolation with which we ourselves are consoled by God. (2 Cor. 1:3–4)

And this:

Bear one another's burdens, and in this way you will fulfill the law of Christ. (Gal. 6:2)

I might add, though, tears are not enough.

If you are a church leader, and your first impulse wasn't to contact or connect with Black churches in the Charleston area to see how you might serve the affected communities, or include time in your service the following Sunday to pray for the families, or even better, discuss with your parishioners the importance of interrogating their own privilege and voting for and against policies that will better serve marginalized communities—if you did not choose to encourage your congregations to stand in solidarity with the Black community against the kind of individual and systemic racism that gives birth to a Dylann Roof, Gregory Bush, or Derek Chauvin—then I would also suggest that you think long and hard about how you are walking out your call.

Because this:

Not many of you should become teachers, my brothers and sisters, for you know that we who teach will
be judged with greater strictness. (Jas. 3:1)

Salvation doesn't come with some kind of transcen-
dence over racist systems. If anything, it comes with a bur-
den to understand how one benefits from those systems
daily, with the next step being an unraveling or dismantling
of the inequity inherent in them.

Exposure, whether of the state of our own hearts or
the larger systems pulling us down, is heavy. The country
can sometimes feel like it is on the brink of civil war. Yet
the one group that should be able to handle what's happening, that should be spiritually armed with both the power
and grace from a Sovereign *and* Warrior God (see Exod.
15), seems to have decided to lay back or be seized by the
enemy. People of faith are certainly caucusing on these
issues. Many white allies have been involved in the fight
for justice. There are always abolitionists among us, and
I'm grateful for that. But today, so many of the white allies
I know of do not identify as Christians—and, dare I say,
for good reason. Where are those who share my faith? And
when does just speaking out even become rote? When simply having a cop car pull up behind my husband, daughter,
and me at a stoplight has me nearly in tears—not because
we're doing anything wrong but because whether we are
doing anything wrong might not matter—well, I wonder
if we are long past white folks posting their outrage in the
form of Black squares on social media and going about their
lives as usual. The next step is probably for every white
person, and especially every white believer, to risk lever-
aging their privilege to dismantle the systems—starting at
their jobs, schools, and yes, churches.

So I wonder if enough are doing *that* work. The data would suggest not. If we are choosing to use the biblical text as a guide, then why aren't most willing to make similar sacrifices as the Acts church? How many of us are willing to be true apostles and have our material lives—and even our physical lives—martyred for standing on the side of love, which ultimately is the side of right?

I understand that, as believers, our first instinct is to pray. It should be. That's a good start. But uh-oh, what happens after we pray? In fact, what exactly are we asking God for? "Thy will be done" is a given. But isn't prayer also about receiving our marching orders? Guidance and direction from the One who sees the end from the beginning? White Christians, are you really ready to ask God to deliver true equality into the hands of people of color in this country, knowing full well what that might require you to do and what that might mean for your own status? Black brothers and sisters, are you ready for the accountability and responsibility that come with justice and equality? If your answers to these questions are yes, then great! However, I suspect that the answer to the next question might be infinitely harder to grasp.

What does God's will regarding this gaping wound of white supremacy in America look like?

What if God's will *is* for the church to take a stand? What if *you*, white Christian, must shout from the rooftops that systemic racism and all its offspring (police brutality, discrimination, educational inequities) are wrong and won't be tolerated, whether it shows up on a flagpole on a state capitol building or in our very own pulpits? What if God's will, Black brothers and sisters, is for you to put down your self-hating "I made it, why can't you?" pseudorighteousness and your "It will get better by and by" complacency and stand alongside those—even the unbelievers—who are marching the streets on behalf of all our futures?

Bottom line: the church as a unified collective, and specifically the white Christians who are part of it, needs to sacrifice whatever narrative we are holding on to that is preventing us from standing up for Black people. Are there white Christians who will put it all on the line for me? Will they stand with me if it means that they will be heckled by those whitewashed tombs they call their own? Like Jesus was heckled by his own? Will white Christians mourn when I mourn and cry when I cry? Though many white Christians might not fully understand why I'm crying, may never completely know my pain, might not even be sure if they think I should be crying . . . the fact that I *am* crying, the fact that my heart aches, the fact that my babies are dying in the streets . . . is that enough for the church as a unified group inclusive of all races and ethnicities to walk alongside me? To champion my healing is to secure its own.

Many church people don't discuss a certain element of stewardship. We often hear the term used in the context of taking care of either financial or natural resources, specifically environmental concerns. We tell people to be good stewards of their money, and in turn we consider ways to save or invest that allow our money to grow in value. We believe we are supposed to take care of the earth—to care for the plants and trees, the animals and fish—and so we recycle and filter our water, and if you're like me, use rain barrels to catch rain so you don't have to use the hose on your garden. These are all obviously great ways to think of stewardship and caretaking. But the one form of stewardship that seems to be constantly overlooked is actually the one way we're going to be able to heal from what racial violence has wrought on us. We are also supposed to take care of each other. Stewardship in the context of humanity requires those of us who consider ourselves people of faith to see the people around us as reflective of the image of God and to care for each other as if we have been summoned to care for God.

I readily admit that the two-way street of relational stewardship becomes incredibly difficult when one has experienced racial violence. I remember meeting a woman in a mothers' group I attended hosted by a church in my neighborhood. The church and the group were predominantly white. Although invited to the group by the small number of Black moms who also attended, I still had such significant skepticism. I was a fairly new mother at the time—my daughter was a toddler—so despite my reservations, I went; frankly, I needed the adult interaction. I entered the group with all my stuff though: the psychological violence I had already experienced from white folks, the church hurt. I felt like I was walking on eggshells at every meeting because I was superconscious of how my Blackness was showing up in the space.

At one group meeting, I met a white woman whom I really enjoyed talking to and whom I recognized as a kind, caring person. She was open to talking about everything from parenting hacks to race, and her questions and comments were always genuine. Talking to her didn't feel like emotional labor as it often does with white women who are trying to be allies. Nevertheless, the damage had already been done. I'd already experienced so much emotional violence at the hands of white people, and especially white Christians, that seeing this woman as being a potential friend was extremely hard despite our camaraderie.

Does this mean I might miss out on opportunities for deep and rich interracial friendships as a result of carrying such pain and skepticism? Most likely. But when you are in a position where a white woman's words or tears or silence could actually end up being the literal death of you or someone you love, it's a thing you're okay with missing. The alternative is so much more devastating.

I think part of the way we heal from the impact of racial violence requires that white people first recognize that many Black folks hold a hesitation, at best—and a healthy fear, at worst—when engaging in fruitful relationships because of the history of potential violence and heartbreak. We understand the way whiteness works in the world and how deeply embedded it is in even the kindest of white folks, so there's always this skepticism or mistrust. It's hard to want to be in relationship with people you feel like at any point in time will prioritize their whiteness over your friendship. If white Christians can simply acknowledge the truth of that and work toward proving themselves racially trustworthy, that would go a long way in facilitating their own healing.

On the other hand, Black folks like myself must reconcile how our history and our present lived experience have fundamentally changed the way we engage with the world and not allow it to rule our hearts and souls in the ways it has—all while also accepting the reality in which we live and not beating ourselves up over it.

I spent a lot of time, especially after my cousin's murder, chastising myself because I chose not to continue some of the relationships I'd begun with the white women in my life. It was mostly fear but also a sense of self-protection as I'd begun to see where these women's loyalties lay during the contentious election and beyond. Plus, I'd always felt safer in the company and sisterhood of Black women anyway, and it was easier to further develop those relationships because of the common ground we shared. But I had to be okay with the fact that healing for me looked exactly like that: rightsizing my faith or what some call "deconstruction," but also choosing to go where I would be loved. It didn't look like rushing out to be friends with the next white woman who came along out of some need to appear like a model of racial reconciliation. Healing meant accepting the reality that trust had not been earned personally or collectively by this particular group, and while open to any relationship, God was not calling me to run after them. Yes, I can look at a person, no matter their race, and identify them as kind—a person who maybe might possibly not be the kind of person who would do something to harm me or my family. But because of my people's historical relationship with white people, and my own experiences of racial violence, I also accept that my feelings are valid and try to move through the world with enough openness that doesn't put me in harm's way. Maybe that calls my faith into question, I don't know. If it does, so be it. All I know is that it is both/and for me, forever and always. I will have enough openness to allow love and joy to be present in my life in whatever form it decides to show up, but will also be attentive and mindful of the potential for harm, intentional or otherwise.

We can heal from racial trauma when we enter into relationships with people, "least of these" or not, and particularly those who are seemingly different from us, with the sole intent to love and care for them. And loving and caring means listening. Loving and caring means opening up our mouths on their behalf when it is absolutely necessary. It means, as the popular unattributed internet quote states, speaking the truth even if our voices shake. The truth is that racism and white supremacy live at the core of all of our systems—including our religious institutions—and that has made living complete lives, filled with all that comes with being human, superchallenging for Black folks. And it's time for it to stop. Stopping might feel like dispossession for white people. Speaking up will feel like betrayal. But that's only because we've been socialized to believe that whiteness is the standard by which all other nouns (people, places, and things) are measured. Removal of whiteness as the standard will certainly feel like a loss, yet in order to reconcile in ways that Christ has taught us, it is a loss that must be embraced for the greater good.

Chapter 5
"WHAT ABOUT CHICAGO?"
*We will heal by choosing accountability
as a precursor to unity.*

When I moved to Chicago in 1997, I was, as they say, as
green as they come. Green, green! I was a recent college
grad who'd left her home state of Kentucky in hopes of
something. That's really the only way that I can describe
it—*something.* I'm not sure exactly what I was looking for,
but I had a firm belief that whatever it was, it wasn't in Kentucky. I rented a Budget van, and with three hundred dollars in my pocket, I drove my twenty-two-year-old self to
the south side of Chicago, where I rented a small studio
apartment half a block from Lake Michigan. After being
there for a year, I finally got a car and was working in sales
while trying to figure out this desire I had for purpose.

As most of us do in our early twenties, I was *living*
my life, which is partially why I thank God every day that
social media didn't exist back then. That may be another
story for another book.

On one particular day, I'd just finished visiting some
friends who attended Chicago State University, a place
where I'd spent a good amount of time the previous summer before graduation, living in their dorms while com-
pleting an internship at Katz Media in Chicago's Loop.
While living there, I met so many people who would be an
integral part of my life for the next few years. I was driving
back to my apartment from the campus at Ninety-Fifth and

Cottage Grove, and I remember coming down Stony Island and then making a right on Seventy-Ninth Street. And just before I got to South Shore Drive, only a few blocks from my apartment, I was stunned by a sight I'll never forget. I saw a car pulled over to the side with two police cars blocking it in: one in front, one behind. Three police officers had surrounded the car with guns drawn. It felt like I'd driven into a scene of *New Jack City*.

One guy in the car had his hands up, but I don't remember the look on his face. I do remember the terror I felt. Strangely enough, no one was around to redirect traffic. I was allowed to cruise slowly past the scene and take it in, which is likely why the image has stuck with me for years.

The police may have felt the need to draw their guns for any number of reasons. The person in the car could have committed some kind of violent crime. It also could have been that the person in the car had done nothing. I suppose that's why I've always wished I could remember the look on the man's face. I somehow feel like seeing his eyes would have told me everything I needed to know about what was really happening in that moment. Still, I know I was more afraid of the police and their guns than I ever was of the man in the car.

Whatever was happening, my sense of safety was shaken that day, as it has been at various points in my life. That same feeling now prevents me from ever feeling comfortable in a grocery store. Back in my twenties, my trepidation came from driving my car down the street to my apartment after visiting my friends, because once again, you just never know what can happen. And yes, I think to a certain extent, when anyone experiences trauma, we all have that feeling. It is, by definition, PTSD. But I'm fairly certain that Black folks walk around holding that level of trauma, that anticipation of violence, in our bodies in a much different way—everything from being pulled over by cops and instead of worrying about getting a ticket or even going to jail, worrying about whether you're going to exit that encounter with your life, to wondering if the next angry white man you encounter is carrying an automatic weapon, causes an entirely different set of emotions and feelings that, when left unhealed, harbors itself in our bodies.

Just as with every other race, some Black people commit crimes, sometimes violent crimes that may necessitate some form of police aggression. Because my information about what was going on in that singular moment of driving by is limited, I can't say what was necessary or not in that instance. But just because this person may have done something that warranted these cops' posture does not mean there aren't a myriad of ways cops abuse their authority and act out violently with Black people. One thing definitely does not mean the other.

Inevitably, when conversations arise about how white people can put an end to racial violence, one hears a reference to "Black-on-Black crime." Many times, these remarks come from white folks trying to balance the scales so that the emphasis isn't solely on race. Sometimes such statements even come from Black people who may have genuine concern about what's happening in their immediate communities but have yet to explore the relationship between the violence itself and the systemic challenges that create the conditions for violence to thrive. In either case, it is a means of deflection intended to counter any call for accountability for racial violence. In her article "Black-on-Black Crime Is a Dangerous Myth," Jameelah Nasheed writes,

A report released by the U.S. Department of Justice
in 2017 found that of all the violent crimes committed between 2012 and 2015, 22.7% were committed
by Black people, and 63% of those were committed
against other Black people. This is in comparison to
44% of all violent crimes committed by white people,
57% of which were committed against other white
people. According to this data, white people commit
crimes against other white people at about the same
rate that Black people do against other Black people.
But despite these numbers, people aren't discussing
the "white-on-white" crime problem. When a white
person commits a crime against another white person, it's just called a crime; race isn't a factor, and
that's intentional. Using language like "Black-on-
Black crime" perpetuates the myth that intraracial
violence is specific to the Black community—a myth
that implies Black people are inherently more violent.
This tactic has been used to justify the mistreatment
of Black people since the abolishment of slavery.[1]

So the bottom line is: Where murder occurs, it's likely that
people will murder people who look like them.

That "Black-on-Black crime" is such a talking point
in conversations regarding racial justice is so strange to
me. It's implying that because one thing is a problem,
something else cannot be equally or even more of a problem. It's the equivalent of saying one shouldn't complain
about racial implications of contaminated water in Flint,
Michigan, that's killing a predominately Black community
because people are also dying of cancer in that same community because of poor eating habits (also very much a systemic issue; see "food deserts"). Two things can be true at

once. There can be problems of violence within a community that need to be addressed, alongside the problems of excessive force and racial violence within the mostly white police departments that are supposed to protect and serve those same communities.

In addition to the Black-on-Black-crime concept being a myth, it is beyond hurtful to hear when you realize that many of the hard things we see within Black communities are a result of the very real systemic violence perpetrated against us as a group. A significant part of the healing journey for many Black people is untangling our own beliefs about who we are as people. Undoubtedly, racism can be internalized. That internalization can often show up as many of the problems we see in Black communities. Those problems, however, are not an out or justification for systemic racism. Those problems are simply the outgrowth of hundreds of years of dehumanization.

Before one brings up Chicago, we have to ask ourselves about how intraracial violence is connected to the abuses of power and brutality that are also commonplace within predominately Black and Brown communities. I suspect that the true link between so-called Black-on-Black crime and police brutality is found in how white supremacy and the systemic institutional inequities born from it actually increase the rate and severity of crime due to the helplessness and despair that any human would feel about their circumstances. In fact, I'd submit that the race-based physical, psychological, and economic violence that are part of this discourse and for which we are working for justice are actually major players in this alleged Black-on-Black violence. That's the connection that we need to examine and not some random deflection that people make in order to stop the conversation about racial violence altogether.

If you want to talk about Black-on-Black crime, that's fine, but talk about it within the context of white supremacy and the structural inequities, poverty, and racial violence that have resulted in these communities. Let's examine the decades-long practice of redlining, which led to the segregation of neighborhoods particularly in places like Chicago. Let's examine the wealth gap between Black and white citizens—even those with the same levels of education. Let's talk about the impact of poverty as a result of these wealth gaps and the underlying reasons for higher unemployment rates in these neighborhoods. Let's take a serious look at underfunded and undersupported schools and limited access to health care in urban communities. And finally, once we've gathered the data, let's see those numbers through a narrative lens. Let's listen to the stories of people trying to stay above water when whole systems want them to drown. Let's hear directly from people who have been placed in a position to have the kind of hopelessness and despair I talked about earlier, with no place to put the pain but still with a need to survive. In these stories, the links are clear. I believe that most Black people absolutely have a desire to lift ourselves out of the prevailing false narrative and align with our ancestral legacy of resilience. It's the reason why those of us who do escape the traps of those stereotypes and generalizations are often lionized within our communities. But something else is equally true. If one is living with trauma and the results of trauma in the body— and on top of that, there is evidence that every major institution around you is designed to make it more challenging for you to get ahead than it is for, say, Chad over *there* in Lincoln Park—then the likelihood of choosing a less acceptable route in order to survive is bound to be greater. It just is. We are human. The good parts of ourselves often have to go underground to survive.

Because some of the "What about Chicago?" commentary comes from other Black people, I'd like to address another relevant aspect of racial violence. There's an old African American saying that goes, "All skinfolk ain't kinfolk." Healing from the violence that comes from internalized racial trauma is likely a larger challenge considering that the enactors on the surface look like our own. But it's no less necessary.

Some of the violence of internalized racism and white supremacy shows up in what is known as "respectability politics." It's not just white folks spouting off about Black-on-Black crime. I've heard this language used by Black folks, within Black institutions and the Black church in particular. Granted, it's usually out of frustration and pain, sometimes even out of a kind of self-determination or need to eschew the perception that white folks are required to help change some of the challenges in our communities. But when this internalized racism shows up in this way, it's not helpful or healing. We can play a key role in helping our own people navigate the results and residue of the internalized lies handed down to us from slavery and colonization—the lies that tell us we are inferior and inherently criminal or that proximity to whiteness means proximity to goodness.

Growing up, I heard sermons and Sunday school lessons implying that there was a certain way for me to move through the world. And some of that, of course, was biblical. It wasn't good to lie. It wasn't good to steal. It wasn't kind or loving to my neighbor to gossip. But then other, more subtle messages were divvied out to us as Black folks about what was necessary to survive and thrive in a world that didn't want that for us. We received messages that all but said that if we dressed a certain way, we wouldn't be perceived as thugs or whores by a police officer or some other, most likely white, person who was in authority. We were supposed to accept these messages, despite however many times someone who was dressed nice and did all the right things still ended up abused or treated poorly by someone in authority. Maybe it was a kind of infusion of hope? A way to hold some belief that we could avoid this kind of violence? I don't doubt that their intentions were another form of survival—a way to hold on to something that felt true, even if reality said it wasn't.

But respectability politics became more than a way to survive the white man's world. It emerged as a tool to create our own stratification within the community. A hierarchy was formed that put the good, amenable Black folks—the ones with the suits and manners and good jobs working for good white folks—on top of some proverbial food chain and anyone else on the bottom, with no consideration that we're all still being eaten. In the same way that some people believe that what a woman wears validates and authorizes sexual violence against her, the same kind of language is used when a young Black man tells someone in the church about the hurtful experience of being stopped by the police. "Well, what did you say? What did you do that made that person do that?" It's a kind of twisted theology, right? Somehow our job is to change our oppressors' mind about us in order to escape violence.

When you blend into the mix an evangelical gospel that holds a misguided interpretation of "Go ye therefore" (see Matt. 28:19 KJV), this idea that we are essentially responsible for the world's moral code and its salvation, you come out with a recipe that allowed for some Black folks to indict others for not falling in line or being godly enough without considering the role that evil systems played in one's circumstances and the need to hold those systems accountable. In my experience, this was a significant driver in my childhood church. As middle school and high school students, we'd go into the public housing complexes—what we called "the projects"—that were behind our church in the west end of Louisville and pass out gospel tracts. We were taught to believe that Jesus would save the people we encountered from their predicament if they wanted it badly enough. With enough prayer, enough coming to church, enough tithing, enough of a deposit of their time and attention into church work, they could reap a harvest that would allow them to escape the systemic nature of their circumstances. Of course, our church leaders could never explain why those who took us up on our offer and did end up coming to our services and doing said church work still lived in those same projects years later.

Was it wrong to tell us to share our faith with other people? I don't think so. There's some truth in the notion of planting good seeds in order to get a good harvest. But an unintentional consequence was that we also took from this the assumption that no other forces were at work. Somehow, all the tract giving, all the salvation offering, all the things we taught that could absolutely save them and help make their lives better didn't align with what we knew awaited most of us when we left church and went to navigate the world. Aside from prayer, we presented no solutions about what people faced elsewhere, including on the job.

In fact, in hindsight, I remember the pained looks of men and women who came to church after a week of what amounted to psychological violence by white bosses and supervisors. We have all kinds of names for that behavior now, "microaggressions" being one term—that subtle feeling of disregard, being made to feel as though you can only go so far, no matter how hard you work; the robbing Peter to pay Paul because minimum wage didn't even cover your rent in subsidized housing; having to be on aid and then being criticized about having to be on aid when none of the dots are connecting; your best being not even remotely good enough. I'm grateful that the parents and grandparents of my childhood church had an altar to cry on when the systemic racism they couldn't control tried to take them out on a daily basis. But I'm also not inclined to judge those who chose other ways to numb that pain.

There are so many layers to the way internalized racism shows up in respectability politics. Anytime we talk about the way human beings choose to survive in the face of trauma, it's a nuanced conversation. That said, I only wish the church, the Black church in particular, could throw aside all these false notions of what will keep us alive and allow the church to be the one place where people can show up as their authentic selves. That has to be the starting point for anything even remotely resembling salvation. Yes, God refines us. God transforms us. God can make us better. But that happens over time. That kind of healing is a process. In the meantime, we shouldn't have to contort ourselves to be any other thing in this world in order to avoid having violence perpetrated against us because of our skin color.

Black and white Christians must both reconcile that respectability is not a fruit of the Spirit. The sad truth is that a Black person can do literally nothing to stop a racist from being racist. The world doesn't have enough bootstraps to pull an entire race out of the depth of multigenerational economic violence. No amount of belted pants, nonhoodied sweatshirts, or closed mouths will keep Black people from dying at the hands of racist white people who believe themselves to be in power.

I'm clear, though, that the internalized enablement of white supremacy is both a survival strategy and a kind of defense mechanism. Most Black folks I know firmly believed that the rights our mothers and fathers fought for during the civil rights movement meant something. We had hope that, in time, we would one day be seen as equal and valuable. But it's been more than fifty years, and we are finding out with every new video and case that maybe that might not be true—at least not to the extent we believed. Some of us are surprised. Some of us aren't. But too many of us have chosen oblivion because it's easier to keep the pain at bay, to not lose our minds. We think that as long as we stay blind and talk about Black-on-Black crime, we can somehow remain respectable and on the good sides of our white friends and fellow believers. As Walter Brueggemann says, we fall into one of two groups: "those who are numb" and "those who despair."[2] The "numb" group insulates themselves so that they don't feel anything. But in order for them to act, they need to be pierced by grief. The "despairing" group feels all the heaviness *and* the powerlessness and just wallows in despair. Both groups need a language that communicates hope for the future.

So what *about* Chicago, my friend? This idea that Black folks should take extraordinary responsibility for what we can do to succeed, without any accountability being laid at the feet of the systemic obstacles that exist, is a one-sided, tone-deaf request at best. Denying and ignoring the systems that impede that responsibility are forms of dehumanization. It's essentially saying we're not allowed to fail in the same ways as white folks. We're not allowed to be stuck. We're not allowed to have all of the things that would literally take out another group. If we were to lay these same overwhelming systemic disparities, the utter dehumanization, at the feet of white people to face on a daily basis, I highly doubt we'd be wondering about why there was hopelessness, despair, and all their devastating consequences. We say, "Hey, I get it." Hell, white folks don't have the same race-related challenges that Black folks do and they are still given passes and concessions for the wretched acts that happen within their communities.

Repairing the residue of enslavement, segregation, redlining, and all the other things that were intentionally put in place to widen the wealth gaps and build playing fields that would never be level, is absolutely the starting point for reconciliation. You can't get to unification without it. And just because there have been those, even many, who have been able to thrive or survive despite never seeing that kind of repair, doesn't take away from the thousands, if not millions who have not. To decide that those relative few are somehow the standard and that those who have not thrived don't deserve an examination of those hindrances is another form of violent dehumanization and is textbook white supremacy.

If we want to heal, then we have to take a look at the injustices of these systems and be willing to dismantle those systems. There's no other way around that. Calling for Black folks to be accountable for crime or any other ill within Black communities by itself is not a problem. As I've said, we can walk and chew gum at the same time. We can address the institutional inequities and also use that work to deal with the problems caused by those inequities. Yet that one-sided call for accountability is usually indicative of an unwillingness to examine all the reasons why these things exist in the first place—and *that* is quite telling.

Unfortunately, calls for the kind of accountability I'm talking about—the kind that says, "Yes, we will work on what's going on within Black communities, but also we will challenge the systems that fuel these problems and try to help create policies that make things more equitable"—are too often seen as divisive and called such outright. When we are in position to establish equity, some white folks don't know what to do with the feelings of loss that arise from their own race-related transgenerational trauma. They don't know what to do with the feeling that something is being taken away from them. They don't know what to do with the notion that any skin privilege they hold can go away.

Again, I realize that words like "advantage" and "privilege" are very sensitive for some white people because they may have grown up in poverty themselves or had some other intersecting identity that created challenges for them. But if we're talking about racial violence, then we're also talking about race-based advantage and the threat some people feel when Black people call for eliminating it.

White people can move a considerable distance toward their own healing by simply not denying those advantages exist. I can draw from my life one maybe even overly simplistic example of that advantage. One of the things I've always wanted to do is take a cross-country trip. I would love to get in a car or train and see pretty much every part of this country from Maine to Seattle, from San Diego to Miami, from D.C. to Denver. When I express this desire to white folks, what I get is 100 percent affirmation:

"You should do it! Go ahead! It's amazing!" My reasons for having not done it, though, generally never cross the minds of those same white people. The truth is, there are still places in this country where people who look like me are simply not welcome. Sundown towns still exist, even if not in name. The Green Book[3] level of planning I'd have to do would steal away some of my excitement as I'd have to plan around those places or simply make sure I could drive quickly enough through them.

I remember being in college and road-tripping to a sorority or fraternity party in another state. It was entirely possible that we'd jump in the car at the University of Kentucky in Lexington and end up at University of Florida in Gainesville. But even then, we understood that there were parts of Kentucky, Tennessee, and Georgia where we would never stop for food, gas, or anything else. There was no stopping. No checking out the historic district. Even then we understood the history of those places and what they saw in us when we drove through. This was confirmed for us the few times we did try to stop for food or gas. The posture and attitude of people toward us were so completely hostile that we left as quickly as possible. The truth is, even the poorest white person would easily move through those same towns without fear of hatred or violence based on the color of their skin. That is a real and clear example of the kind of advantage and privilege that exist. Calling that out isn't divisive. If anything, it is a call for healing, a call for recognition that, "Hey, this wound hurts—every day."

Any individual white person we meet may not be the direct cause of these wounds we carry. But that same white person does continue to benefit from the advantages and privileges that open these wounds. The question is, are you the kind of white person who would be willing to give up some of those things that indirectly keep my wounds open, so that my wounds can ultimately heal? I am certainly not putting the full healing of Black folks on white people's shoulders. That is by far *not* what I'm saying. White folks are not responsible for Black folks' healing at the root. In fact, our resilience is legendary. We have been healing for generations without white folks' intervention. But if we want to see a healing in our country, in personal and collective relationships, in the trauma that comes from the violence that this country has wrought over hundreds of years against Black and Indigenous folks, white folks en masse are going to have to take some real actions—ones that may require sitting squarely in the discomfort that comes with being challenged—in order for that to happen.

Chapter 6

FADING EMPATHY

*We will heal by affirming that there are
many routes to where we must go,
but love must pave every path.*

I am at a critical juncture in writing this book. It's a place I
inevitably arrive whenever I'm working on any project.
I look at the thousands and thousands of words I've com-
posed, and I think half of it is trash, and half of it still needs
a lot of work. But the feeling I have right now is just a bit
different because wrapped into my normal self-deprecation
at this stage of my writing is a kind of incredulous feeling.
*Am I really writing a whole book challenging people to recog-
nize that the racial violence Black people experience is "really
bad" and that healing is needed across the board?* When I
break it all the way down, that's what it feels like in this
moment—that I'm writing a book that is outlining all the
ways that racial violence is pervasive and traumatic. Why in
the world am I doing that?

I've built so much of my writing career trying my best
to de-center the white gaze, to emphasize that no aspect of
Black folks' humanity requires validation from white people—even when our systems try to snatch our lives from us,
we prevail because God, in a myriad of forms, has always
been with us. If I'm honest, I don't want to care about what
white people, Christian or otherwise, think about the racial
violence I've experienced. I'm not even sure if *I* should.
Yet at the same time, I know as humans we are all deeply

connected and there has to be some willingness to engage even the worst of us if we want to carry on.

I'm not terribly interested in convincing white people that I am worthy of safety from racial violence. I'm just as worthy as anyone. Black people are just as worthy as any other group to live lives that are not threatened at every turn because of our skin color. I'm more interested in figuring out the ways we can all heal from the violence that has already occurred and that still occurs because our systems continue to function the way they were designed.

So, right in the middle of this narrative, I feel a push to shift away from this notion that I have to teach anyone to denounce racial violence. For me, that is a given. If you call yourself a Christian, a believer, then violence should rarely be the answer to any conflict. And if you believe that there is ever a reason to employ racial violence as a means to wield power over Black and Brown folks, however small the act is in your eyes, then I can write nothing that will prompt you toward the level of empathy one needs to enact change.

My goal has always been for this book to center the healing needed to overcome what racial violence has wrought in our communities, both white and Black. To the world, this country, there has to be a conversation about the ways in which violence, racial violence in particular, is insidious and tears away at a person's humanity—and not just for the marginalized. It's not just Black and Brown folks who are impacted. It's not just Black people who need to heal. It's white people too. In Kellie Stallard Watson's words,

> My experience is that white people cannot relate or understand the experiences Black people have

because of racism, bias, and hate. It is not their experience, so sharing stories or telling them our experiences is not always believable to them. Acknowledgment of our racist and violent history and the systematic and institutional racism and discrimination that advantages them, and hurts and kills us, is a start. It is not about their white guilt or fragility but understanding that the racial trauma and violence Black people live with is harmful for everyone and that continuing this in our systems and institutions is a detriment to our future.

I would argue that white people as a whole have experienced a severe erosion of empathy as a result of embracing and accepting whiteness and the ugly that comes with it. The timeline for that erosion seems to line up with the horrific experiences of Black and Brown people on these shores. On the one hand, the clear evils of enslavement indicate that even back then these white people didn't have much empathy, but there are also those who simply watched enslavement happen or accepted it as a societal norm. There are the clear evils of inequality and segregation that indicated a lack of empathy for Black people in the Jim Crow era, and then there are the white people who didn't necessarily put those laws in place or even agree with them, but accepted them as a fact of life and benefited from them. In both instances, the latter group seems to have had their empathy eroded over time—possibly due to desensitization.

We cannot ignore how the impact of the increasing and excessive exposure to violence in general and against Black people specifically has created desensitization. But I do admit that when my rage and sorrow reach debilitating levels, I can't help but wonder if, from the standpoint of epigenetics, the apathy and even outright resistance some white folks today demonstrate when faced with racial violence against Black people is simply a function of our present-day brutality resonating with some part of that white person's DNA that secretly supports the violence. We explore that more in the next chapter.

Empathy means having the ability to acknowledge another's pain, understand where a person is coming from, or at the very least, being able to sit with someone in their hurt and pain and connect with that person as another human being. Empathy often means that, in some capacity, we are able to put ourselves in another's shoes and imagine what it might feel like if we were dealing with the same issues. And now that empathy and vulnerability are mainstream subjects, plenty of definitions for those buzzwords are available. People are talking about these topics in really wonderful ways—even in order to get people to understand what's necessary to drive forward equity and social justice movements. But one challenge is people's assumption that, barring being a psychopath, we all have empathy. Popular TikTok philosophers say we just need to get people to see that they need to be more empathetic, or vulnerable enough to tap into their empathy, in order to deal with any number of societal ills.

But when it comes to race, we may have to reckon with the fact that the *capacity* for empathy for many white people in particular has been diminished if not erased. I wonder about the expectation that white people can be exposed to or perpetrate racial violence of any form regularly—be inundated with images of Black and Brown folks being violently treated, generation after generation, for hundreds of years—and not be desensitized to it. And if, alongside this violence, society assumes your inherent superiority or you subconsciously believe that your privilege and advantages are reasonable or warranted, then how does that not further the gap between you and the person or group for which you're now supposed to have empathy? Is it even possible for you to sit with them in their pain knowing that their pain exists because of your own ancestral legacy?

At a micro level, I do believe that an individual white person can feel pity for an individual Black person in their sphere of relationships. There is absolutely the capacity to say, "I feel sorry for you," or "Let me donate some money to that group addressing that really bad thing I don't want to think about." But we all know that pity is not the same as empathy. Throwing money at a problem, as much as it is likely appreciated, does not actively drive human healing. Standing alongside someone, standing in their proverbial shoes, putting your own body on the line is an entirely different thing.

As I write this I'm reminded of the rage I felt when I learned the whole story of my cousin's murder. When Gregory Bush exited the grocery store, after already shooting Maurice Stallard, he crossed paths with another white man who was also armed and, after seeing what was happening, had pulled out his own gun. This murderer allegedly said to the man, "Oh, don't worry, whites don't kill whites," and continued to the parking lot where he shot and killed my cousin.

I remember hearing this and thinking to myself, So, wait, that armed bystander heard this *and put his gun away?* What would it have taken for this white man to understand that danger was imminent—hearing what Bush said and knowing Black people were in the direction where he was heading—to be willing to put his own body on the line to prevent continued violence? It was actually another Black man, also armed, who chased Bush after he shot Cousin Vickie and sped out of the lot. This Black man, who could have easily been a target of police for simply carrying a gun, legal or not, chose to try to do something, anything, to help.

I can't help but wonder, would the outcome, at least for my cousin, have been different had there been the same level of empathy from that initial white witness as from the Black witness. I understand that other things could have been at play. He could have been in shock. The events of that moment could have moved really fast. I don't want to blame this person necessarily. However, I don't think you can have a conversation about empathy without acknowledging that if a person does not see someone who's different from them—in this case Black people—as equally worthy of life and protection, then that just might affect how quickly that person reacts to racial violence when it shows up nearby.

How do you get a person to empathize with someone they may subconsciously not even believe is as valuable as themselves? I'm not sure you can. Consider what Jesus said about this.

> Jesus replied with a story: "A Jewish man was traveling from Jerusalem down to Jericho, and he was attacked by bandits. They stripped him of his clothes, beat him up, and left him half dead beside the road.
>
> "By chance a priest came along. But when he saw the man lying there, he crossed to the other side of the road and passed him by. A Temple assistant walked over and looked at him lying there, but he also passed by on the other side.

"Then a despised Samaritan came along, and
when he saw the man, he felt compassion for him.
Going over to him, the Samaritan soothed his
wounds with olive oil and wine and bandaged them.
Then he put the man on his own donkey and took
him to an inn, where he took care of him. The next
day he handed the innkeeper two silver coins, telling
him, 'Take care of this man. If his bill runs higher
than this, I'll pay you the next time I'm here.'

"Now which of these three would you say was a
neighbor to the man who was attacked by bandits?"
Jesus asked.

The man replied, "The one who showed him
mercy."

Then Jesus said, "Yes, now go and do the same."
(Luke 10:30–37 NLT)

Whenever we talk or read about the story of the good
Samaritan, it's usually focused on the one person who
stopped to help the individual who has been robbed and
devastated, and is otherwise in a really bad way on the side
of the road. But I would submit that the first two who passed
by tell us a lot about the way assumed superiority works in
traumatic circumstances. Those first two passersby, a priest
and a temple assistant, ironically part of the religious order
of the day, didn't believe that the hurt person was worthy
of assistance. He held no value to them, and therefore they
couldn't empathize with him long enough to stop and help.
Ironically, it took someone who was also marginalized to
see this person's pain, recognize it, and do what was necessary to help, despite the person being different from them.

If we're talking about what's necessary for healing the
pain and trauma of Black folks, as well as dealing with the

residue of white-supremacist thinking in white folks, it's important to start with how one may perceive Black people. Can a white person be truly honest about that and really interrogate what society has taught them to believe about a whole group of people without making it the responsibility of that same group to educate them?

White people have to be able to reckon with the truth of Black people's lived experience as a whole, but also within their own spheres of influence. The question then becomes, have the Black lives I've touched changed? If we are examining this historically, then yes, absolutely, there has been progress for Black people as a whole. But just because I walk two steps forward in the three miles I've got to go to get home—progress, for sure—doesn't get around the fact that I still have a long way to go.

Vast disparities remain—enormous gaps in our systems. So, if empathizing with Black folks means white people truly see us as equally human and as valuable as any-one else, then one of the first steps needed for healing is to ensure that the systems reflect that fact. Unfortunately, we're seeing so far that this, by and large, is not what's hap-pening. In fact, the recent doubling down on the racial vit-riol and violence not only hurts the marginalized but offers no opportunity for transformation or empathic evolution for those who, openly or by virtue of their silence, remain complicit with it.

The theology that many people are attempting to create around their lack of empathy is even more devastating. Some have bought into a bad theology that says empathy is wrong, even sinful, because holy compassion would demand that they set aside their doctrine—the very thing that needs investigation. They've convinced themselves and others that empathy is some kind of idolatry—a way to put the love and care of each other above the love of God—as opposed to the very core of God's intention for creation.

Calling empathy sin or some type of aberration of what God intends for us is borderline demonic, but it's also another way that separation is being allowed. It is not divisive to empathize and care for the marginalized. It is not divisive to challenge those who don't. No, division happens when you refuse to see as human, as deserving, the people to whom you're being asked to show empathy. What causes division is when you attempt to take away someone's humanity through this act of subtle violence. Yes, stealing away empathy, withholding your compassion from a person, are acts of violence too. If we saw that happening between a parent and child, we would be angry and likely would remove that child from their parent, or at the very least, address it in some kind of way. That parent would be put on notice that the way they are neglecting their child, by not providing empathy, is unacceptable.

Yet at a collective global level, that is what happens to Black and Brown folks every single day. It's often not always some big lack of compassion or forgoing of empathy. It is the everyday dehumanization that occurs and chips away at us.

Numerous Scripture verses in both the Old and New Testaments demonstrate the power and necessity of empathy and compassion. In an attempt to trick him or to somehow catch him in a lie, the Pharisees asked Jesus which is the greatest commandment from the law of Moses. Jesus is very clear that it's all about love. He replies, "'You must love the Lord your God with all your heart, all your soul, and all your mind.' This is the first and greatest commandment.

A second is equally important" (Matt. 22:37–39 NLT). "Equally" is so key here. Jesus makes loving your neighbor as yourself the equivalent to loving God. Just as important as loving God your creator is loving your neighbor as yourself, and every other law hangs on these two. Yes, maybe people have different definitions of what loving your neighbor means, but if we were to really examine that word "love," either *philia* (friendship or affection) or *agape* (unconditional or sacrificial love)—embedded in both are what we now know about empathy and vulnerability: being able to sit with another, to walk alongside someone as they heal and grieve. Essentially, Jesus hangs on this idea of love our sense of morality, our sense of what is right or wrong, our desire to know the next good thing to do.

Western evangelical Christians have created a hierarchy that is not present in anything that Jesus models for us. They say that loving God with all your soul and all your mind is the most important. And then *underneath* that, in a total misreading of Scripture, comes loving your neighbor. I think the reason for this theological misstep is that then one can logically say that if loving your neighbor causes you, for some reason, not to love your God with all your heart and mind, then loving your neighbor takes second place. But that's actually not what Jesus says, nor is it what he models for us. He says that as much as you say you love God, equal to that love of God with all your soul, mind, and heart is your love of your neighbors. These two actions are in relationship with each other.

I honestly believe that if we embrace that "equally" piece, we'd have fewer people flying Confederate flags in the name of God and country (weird, since the Confederacy lost). In fact, this reading of Scripture would mean that much of what white evangelicals do sociopolitically in the name of God and country would clearly not be or feel anywhere near the vein of loving one's neighbor and would create some dissonance. Love must be our guiding force. But even in that, we must be clear about what love looks and feels like. I can't emphasize enough just in my own experience how critical embodiment is to our understanding of the manifestation of racial trauma and violence. Resmaa Menakem, author of *My Grandmother's Hands: Racialized Trauma and the Pathway to Mending Our Hearts and Bodies*, helps us with this:

> We've tried to teach our brains to think better about race. But white-body supremacy doesn't live in our thinking brains. It lives and breathes in our bodies.
>
> Our bodies have a form of knowledge that is different from our cognitive brains. This knowledge is typically experienced as a felt sense of constriction or expansion, pain or ease, energy or numbness. Often this knowledge is stored in our bodies as wordless stories about what is safe and what is dangerous. The body is where we fear, hope, and react; where we constrict and release; and where we reflexively fight, flee, or freeze. If we are to upend the status quo of white-body supremacy, we must begin with our bodies.[1]

God created us to be in community with each other. We are interdependent people. It's the reason why there's that report revealing that if you deprive a baby of touch, as was observed in an orphanage—no hugs, kisses, or compassion when they fall down—then the baby becomes sick. A baby becomes physically and mentally despondent without love and compassion as opposed to a child who is nurtured. Loving care creates safety and health.

Knowing what love and joy and peace feel like in your body really gives you access. It is key to understanding what those things mean in your spirit and in your heart. Because too many of us have not done the work necessary to unpack the issues that, over time—whether from our childhoods or everyday experiences—prevent us from experiencing love, we find ourselves articulating this idea of loving our neighbors without actually knowing exactly what that love feels like in our bodies. Is it a warmth spreading from the center of our chests? A calm that seems to tingle and spread in our head and face? Once I figured out what love felt like physically to me, I was inclined to make sure everyone around me experienced it also, in their own ways. Embodiment led to an expansion of my empathy.

Just a taste of God's love will have you hunting for another taste. It's enticing that way, which makes me think that maybe, just maybe, *that's* the good news we should be spreading. Maybe demonstrative love such as Christ modeled for us on the cross is our salvation and not some rote recitation of the Romans Road.[2] What if white Christians were able to disconnect from the legacy of violence they've inherited and able to somehow transform that legacy into extreme love for the marginalized, the people for whom Jesus showed up? Because if we really do claim Jesus as our model, then we'd show up for them too.

One of the challenges I faced when I lost my cousin was knowing that her story would go away. It's the nature of the social-media-driven, twenty-four-hour news cycle, and it angered me fiercely. Sure enough, within a few days of her murder, the Tree of Life Synagogue shooting occurred right outside of Pittsburgh. That horrific tragedy, in which eleven people were shot and killed in their place of worship, reminded me of what happened to the Charleston Nine and to the four little girls in Birmingham. We once saw churches and synagogues and mosques as safe places, and now they aren't. That hurts. But this story also moved my cousin's murder out of the news cycle, and as much I understood why that happened, I didn't know what to do with all of my feelings about it. I needed her name to be shouted every day until there was justice. Couldn't she be the last hashtag for a while? The answer was no.

The racial injustice and violence that have received so much visibility in the last decade, thanks to a smartphone in every pocket, are not new. Black and Brown people have been experiencing brutality at the hands of whites since Columbus figured out he wasn't actually in India and those thousands of people already living here weren't Indians. Fortunately, social media has been able to shine a big, bright, ugly light on what has been a common experience for those in Black communities. Social media, with all its ills, has served as a technological mirror for our society—a mirror that reflects a truth so ugly that so many white people in the faith have chosen to sweep it under the rug.

This truth reveals to some that, while they worship and serve in cities that might be highly diverse, their immediate worlds are not. This truth reveals that most believe that the Black church and a few select white activists have the responsibility to deal with all that civil rights stuff. This truth reveals that some still have antiquated notions of how to engage those who are different (bringing Lecrae to a once-a-year youth conference but never truly connecting with the demographic he represents does *not* count). This truth also exposes the inner workings of individual hearts: hearts that don't have a problem serving rice to the inner-city poor at a soup kitchen but who wouldn't dream of inviting those same people into their homes, hearts that don't have a problem with integrated schools or pools as long as the white folks are never outnumbered—and their daughters and sons don't bring "one" home.

When people who call themselves Christ-followers stop really seeing people and decide to replace human beings with stereotypes and caricatures gathered from a biased and agenda-driven media, it makes the decision to not stand for right seem, well, right. When Eric Garner becomes just another lazy Black guy standing on the corner selling cigarettes—instead of a hard-working father talking to friends in his community and making a couple of extra dollars for his family . . . and that image is used to justify his death . . . there is, without a doubt, a deep heart problem. It's got to go beyond just "those people" wanting social justice. Those people are your brothers and sisters in humanity. Just as the visibility of marchers at Selma being firehosed, beaten, and bitten by police dogs helped some white people in other parts of the country consider assisting the civil rights movement, the visibility of racial injustice and violence today via social media has amplified Black voices and made some white people consider joining the present-day movement for Black lives.

That said, there is absolutely a downside to so much media exposure and amplification of the dehumanization, brutality, and violence that Black people experience. Beyond desensitization, there is the psychological and physiological impact, particularly for Black folks, of seeing dead Black bodies lying in the street. I'm thinking about the tendency for a Black mother to transpose the face of her own child on the images of those men and women—or the Black father who hesitates, if only for a millisecond, when he steps out the door for work. It's an interesting paradox that this violence is something that we unfortunately have become accustomed to seeing and experiencing (desensitization), and yet underneath our skin we know it's something we will never get used to (trauma).

Running away from the hard stuff—the stuff that makes us uncomfortable, the stuff that challenges our notions of who we and others are, the systems we work and live in, and what God is calling us to do—is a natural, human tendency. It is a battle we face historically and in the present day. All wranglings with the flesh are. But the one thing that usually gives "right" and "love" the edge in our internal wars is this sense that we belong to each other, that we live in this outpost of Eden together and that even the worst of us is connected to us somehow.

Yet here we are. Men, women, and children are being murdered, and for the most part, the church is absent.

Well, we aren't totally absent. Many of us will show up when those who are dealing with this pain, this generations-long disenfranchisement, turn to rioting. When we feel threatened, when there's a possibility that the rage will hit too close to our safe havens and disrupt our status quos, then some will have a whole lot to say.

Rev. Dr. Martin Luther King's response to such "sudden concern" is more powerful than anything I could write:

> It is not enough for me to stand before you tonight and condemn riots. It would be morally irresponsible for me to do that without, at the same time, condemning the contingent, intolerable conditions that exist in our society. These conditions are the things that cause individuals to feel that they have no other alternative than to engage in violent rebellions to get

attention. And I must say tonight that a riot is the language of the unheard.[3]

I'm not sure that humans were made to hold so much pain at once. On the one hand, I get it. I'd like to believe that we are limitless. Our capacity to deal with loss and grief is pretty much unknown, right? Whatever you believe about how mankind came about, it's clear we didn't create ourselves. And if we believe God created us, then only God alone knows our emotional and psychological capacity. But in the same vein, if I think about the created human body, the clear limitations of it, I can't help but wonder if we were ever meant to hold the levels of information, and ultimately pain, that we take in daily via the internet. Every day we are holding not just our own stories but stories of sometimes hundreds if not thousands of other people—stories like Marcus's and Sean's and Kellie's, who shared with me how she's managing her own grief:

> I was a very private person. To have to grieve publicly was/is very difficult. People have in their minds how you are supposed to behave and react. As I stated, the impact was felt across this community. I have to be prepared at all times for his death to come up. I really wish people would remember how he lived, not how he died. I am always on guard emotionally and spend a lot of time making others feel better and comforted about what happened. I am in therapy and was not before this. My life has changed dramatically, and sometimes coping with that is difficult. It is overwhelming. There is so much to do, so much that I am responsible for that, at times, I do not even know how I feel or have time to deal with it. Sometimes I

feel numb. The news can be very triggering, and as I stated, there is not a day that passes that I do not think about my dad. I miss him so much, it hurts. There is a gap where he should be. I do not feel like I have had time to myself to grieve.

I'm a proponent of storytelling. I believe in the power of giving air to both pain and joy. I was definitely the kind of kid who wanted to know all the stories, listening around the corner as my elders would spill the tea about the family or other members of our community. Even now, I want to know all the stories, whether it's in the form of articles, books, or films; whether it's an essay or somebody's aunt telling me a tale via her Instagram stories. Whatever shape or form the story takes, I want it. But along with all those stories comes the weight they carry. Every story—a different journey, a different weight. Being inundated with thousands of stories a day or a week—many attached to various emotions and traumas—can take its toll. Those burdens become too heavy, and we end up weighed down in ways that don't allow us to serve anyone.

For Black people, I think by trying to hold it all—our personal pain, the hurt of our community, and traumas of the world—something is happening to us, both individually and collectively. We are breaking down. That breakdown causes us to act out against each other in both large and small ways—and that acting out creates more stories, more pain, and more trauma, to which, once again, we're all paying attention, and on and on.

I wonder if part of healing from racial violence for Black folks means that we let some of the stories go and embrace stillness—not because of a lack of empathy or compassion, but because doing so would allow us to step back into a space where we create boundaries around what we take in and be useful to our cause.

I remember when the recording of George Floyd's murder hit social media. It took me a very long time to watch that video, way longer than people might think— probably a few months—even then I don't think I watched it in its entirety. I couldn't. Something happens to my body when I watch videos like that. When I finally did see the whole recording, my body trembled. I shook and shook and couldn't make it stop. The welling of tears behind my eyes, even now as I write this, makes it so, so hard for me to hold those kinds of images because it's a pain that rings a bell in my soul that reminds me of my cousin's murder, which reminds me of Sandra Bland, which reminds me of Trayvon Martin, which reminds me of Emmett Till, which reminds me. . . .

It all runs together and becomes too heavy, so when another hashtag takes over my timeline, sometimes I have to be still. Obviously I support and stand in solidarity with the families of these victims. I will do anything I can to use my gifts to help amplify the names of those who succumb to state-sanctioned and other white-supremacist-influenced violence. But I also have to make sure that I'm not creat- ing more mental health challenges for myself as a result of taking it all in in large doses. It's hard, because I know inti- mately the importance of sounding the alarm. I want white folks in particular, and white Christians especially, to know about the damage being done to my community. I need to say those names loudly and regularly. Because I do empa- thize. Because I can put myself in their shoes—and despite the tension that results in saying those names loudly every single day or week and knowing how it tears my insides apart.

That's the violence that comes from the violence. I don't think I was made to hold all of that. I believe that because of the way my brain feels. So where are the white people who claim Christ and have wrestled their empathy back from their own murderous ancestral legacy? Will they carry some of this? Nowadays we hear, especially in antiracism teaching, Black folks saying, "White people, you take care of this. You created this system, you and the generations before you benefit from this system, so you fix it. You dismantle it. Don't ask us. We're healing." But I'm not sure there's been any rush to take up this mantle of empathy, which is frustrating to say the least. As James Baldwin said in an interview featured in the documentary *James Baldwin: The Price of the Ticket*, "What is it you want me to reconcile myself to? . . . You always told me it takes time. It has taken my father's time, my mother's time, my uncle's time, my brothers' and my sisters' time, my nieces' and my nephews' time. How much time do you want for your 'progress'?"[4]

As Vickie's son, my cousin Sean Jones, said, "Black folks are a resilient people. Eventually, we will get tired of being poked, and will begin poking back."

Black folks have shared our lived experiences until we're blue in the face. White people can acknowledge those experiences—accept them, honor them, do something about them—or not. But a shift is underway. White folks are being challenged to decide whether they're going to truly be allies, accomplices, and enactors in changing this world we live in or if they will just, per usual, wait for Black folks to march again or rise up again or somehow figure out some way to break all of the ceilings and all the walls . . . again.

Newsflash: We're tired.

Chapter 7

THE REAL CAUSES
OF WHITE VIOLENCE

*We will heal by embracing the process of healing
and all that we uncover on the journey.*

One of the things I wrestled with when it came to the verdict that ultimately put the person who murdered my cousin behind bars for the rest of his life was the attempt to attribute the racism that drove his horrific act solely to his mental health. I'm certainly not ignorant of the fact that there are outlier instances when someone has not taken medication or has struggled and, therefore, acts out violently. I won't pretend that doesn't exist. But I also know that when it comes to white people who are accused and then ultimately proven to have murdered Black and Brown folks with racist intent, other white people too often rush to position it as mental illness or shape it so that we aren't having the conversation about what's inherent or passed down generationally in white people. It's like some are afraid to say that maybe the perpetrators of racial violence are as sane as anyone else when they commit these acts, that their actions are driven by racism and not necessarily by any mental challenge.

Mental illness across the spectrum is not foreign to me. From my own battles with anxiety and depression, to family members who struggle with bipolar disorder or paranoid schizophrenia, I have been touched by, or have had the opportunity and privilege to experience being around, people who live with mental health challenges, enough to know that they would never murder someone as a result of any of their symptoms. It feels terribly ableist then to write off an act of racial violence as related to mental health, because that conclusion lends itself to the assumption that anyone who struggles with mental health issues has the equal capacity to act out in racially violent ways—which just hasn't proven to be the case. In fact, if it were true that most racial violence stems from mental illness, then the inverse would also be true. I'd argue that with the amount of trauma Black people have faced, and the subsequent mental health challenges that come with it, if this was true, there would have long ago been a revolt like this country and this hemisphere has never seen. White folks, to be frank, would be strung up everywhere.

Making the actors in racial violence the victims of mental illness is scapegoating the very real systemic inequities and white-supremacist philosophies that feed the superiority and entitlement some white people feel when it comes to Black and Brown folks. It is just another example of only addressing the fruit and not the root. The fruit is the fact that we have people walking around here who believe themselves to be better than me or people who look like me because they are white. And they have been indoctrinated by a society that says their whiteness is the standard and takes precedence in any and every instance.

There are already so many stigmas that exist around mental health. We do a disservice to people who are living with mental health challenges when we try to make racism just another DSM category. I was once a proponent of that, but after living through the last five years, it now just doesn't feel right to me. Like Zora Neale Hurston, I too believed that you had to be mentally ill to not engage with all the wonderful, glorious things about Black people:

Sometimes, I feel discriminated against, but it does not make me angry. It merely astonishes me. How can any deny themselves the pleasure of my company? It's beyond me.[1]

I suppose it took being on the other side of the pain caused by racial violence to realize that something else, something deeper than "he was off his meds," is at work. There are numerous problems with writing off racism and racial violence as mental health issues. It makes sense that we do this, though. As human beings, I think we tend to look for easy outs. We also desire to make sense of something that is nonsensical: a person kills another person because of the color of their skin. While this topic is terribly nuanced because, in some cases, mental health *can* be an issue, it's also incredibly damaging for Black people to have the horrible deaths of family members and friends written off as isolated incidents when the racism motivating the perpetrators is so systemic. The biggest flaw in this reasoning is evidence revealing that most don't arrive at racial violence haphazardly.

If we choose to identify white folks as also having transgenerational trauma as a result of that indoctrination into violence via their ancestral legacy of slavery, colonization, and genocide, then maybe we do have to make room for the fact that this violence is born from that trauma.

In a way, I think it might do a disservice to Black folks to focus solely on the way our trauma has been passed down, without thinking about what has occurred in the bloodlines of white people that makes violence so easily processed as an option for affirming their self-designated superiority. Even passive participation in the degradation of an entire group of people—including enslavement,

segregation, and ongoing macro- and microaggressions—
inevitably creates desensitization. White people have a
pathological need to make sense of what's clearly a violation
of human rights and to find justifications for the violence.
This showed up when white people who watched the video
of George Floyd's murder still found a way to question
whether Floyd's behavior somehow justified the behavior
of police.

I'm not even sure it's a conscious act at this point for
many white people who do this. The need for "more information" feels like it's only applied when Black and Brown
people are the victims, and that's very telling. Essentially,
this thinking says that if a person is Black and something
bad happens to them at the hands of a white person, then
somehow the Black person is responsible. And if one has
been trained, over time, via generations of false narratives,
to believe that somehow this group of people is inferior,
savages even, then the justification feels reasonable. The
empathy deficit is therefore very much part of the transgenerational trauma that has been passed down to white folks
in America. This is not to say that the trauma of every single
white person descended from those who lived through the
legal transatlantic slave trade here in the Americas or whose
families have embraced the benefits of conferred whiteness
as European immigrants, shows up in the same way. But
shifting the conversation to an examination of whiteness
is nevertheless extremely important. Transgenerational
trauma isn't just something that impacts marginalized
people. As much as a reckoning is needed, healing must
result from it. The question is whether white folks will be
willing to heal, even if that healing means a loss of status,
possible reduction in wealth, and certainly the sacrifice of

what they've always believed about themselves and their whiteness.

Writer and educator Stacey Patton began to unpack some of the latter while conducting research for a new book, and it blew my mind when she shared some of her findings on Facebook.

I had always assumed that lynching was the culmination of a distinctly anti-Black form of dehumanization triggered by post-Reconstruction-era politics, sexual hysteria, economic malaise, and other regional factors.

But it is deeper than that. We can't talk about lynchings without exploring intergenerational trauma, genetic memory, parental attachment, love, bonding, connection, and white family gatherings and the link to racial violence.

What I am learning is that trauma can be inherited. You can inherit the unconscious patterns of thoughts, feelings, and behaviors of your ancestors. If your ancestors faced harsh environments you can inherit the ways they responded to life-threatening conditions. Those responses then become tools for protection and survival.

So generations of white bodies and minds have been shaped by plagues, wars, starvation, religious persecution, domination, land theft, public terror, and other harsh experiences of their ancestors in Europe. Those whites who came to the American colonies inherited and carried the terror, hypervigilance, grief, and rage in their bodies. They had a deep desire to relieve the pain and trauma from their early childhood experiences and so they projected all that onto the bodies of Indigenous folks and Black people through genocide, enslavement, and racist serial killings.

And so when we get to lynching scenes centuries later, what we are witnessing is white bodies unconsciously recalling terror and trauma from another time when they had to go into survival mode and adapt to stress.

When we see them torturing and destroying Black children, they are projecting all that unhealed ancestral rage and terror they inherited onto us. In other words, generations of white racists have held Black folks responsible for the full breadth of fear and suffering that we had nothing to do with.

More than anything, the severity of this issue lies in how we name the source, and the ways in which we enforce laws based on this understanding. Is relating the acts of racial violence to the inherent generational trauma in white people essentially a get-out-of-jail-free card? When a murderer like the one who killed my cousin can plead guilty by reason of insanity in order to avoid the death penalty, what does that really mean? And where are we putting the onus, the responsibility: on the person or on the uninvestigated trauma in their DNA? Again, acknowledging transgenerational trauma in white folks is by no means an escape hatch, nor an excuse for lack of accountability. But it can be a starting point toward ripping up the source of the violence we see.

An intricate path leads a person to pull out a gun and kill a Black person in the park, in the line of a grocery store, or walking into a church. A winding path takes a person to that point. You have to have been told that these individuals are a threat to you or you have to somehow believe that these people's lives don't matter as much as yours or you must have been indoctrinated within a system that says that you must protect yourself solely on the basis of your whiteness. You must believe that by enacting violence against these individuals, you are somehow doing exactly that—protecting whiteness, the thing you've been taught all along to do.

The motivation to take someone's life based on race comes from all the things I've been talking about in this book. It comes from an environment, a system that implies, if not says directly, that whiteness should be protected at all costs—that a threat to that whiteness exists at all. More diversity, inclusion, and equity become evidence that something is being taken away. That feeling of power and authority slipping away, I imagine, creates a target in the perpetrators' mind. Even if I were to concede that mental illness causes the violent, psychopathic reaction—and I still think it's ableist to do so—I don't think we can avoid how systemic racism and white supremacy plant the seed and create the target where that uncontrolled violence will land.

One of the ways I've been able to nurture my own healing and curate a space to pray, meditate, and do my healing work is through gardening. The gardening process is my way of connecting to other kinds of creation and attempting to get a peek into the mind of God. I'm also drawn to the divine creative power that the garden represents. It reflects what I hope to do in other parts of my life.

I started gardening maybe ten years ago, but got really intensely into it within the last five or six years. Every year, when we were in our first home, I had to have a garden box or something for growing my fruits and veggies. I'll never forget what happened in 2019 when I decided to plant some yellow squash. I planted the seeds at the appropriate time in the season, which is not always possible with the way the weather fluctuates in the mid-Atlantic region. But they took root and started growing like wildfire, to the extent that the plants practically took over. Some of that was my fault. I'd been planting things too closely, so the plants crowded each other and then started vining into the tomato and eggplant boxes.

Nevertheless, the squash blossoms were beautiful. Then one day I happened to go out and see a little tiny bug crawling on the large leaves. *Okay.* I didn't think too much about it. I see bugs on plants all the time. I know that some bugs are beneficial and others are not, and I'm not always aware of which are which. A couple of days later, I went back out to see a massive number of these bugs. Hundreds. Still, I'm like, *Okay. Surely these little bugs aren't going to be too much of a problem with all this squash, right?*

I did a little bit of research and asked people in my Facebook gardening groups what to do, and I soon learned that these were vine borers, or squash bugs, and they would attack my squash. I was so upset. I was really looking forward to having this huge harvest of squash, but all I could see was these bugs taking over. I did everything I could to try to save my crop. I sprayed it with Neem oil, thinned out the vines, and created a myriad of concoctions I was told would kill the bugs. And it did kill some of them, but not all of them. Over time, I watched my plants disintegrate.

Some squash did grow—we probably got two or three actual squash out of it. The rest of the blossoms, however, were just devoured—so far gone, there was really no way I was going to be able to salvage anything because the bugs had indeed taken over. These vine borers were an invasive enemy that had attacked my plants to the extent that the only thing left to do was pull up all of the vines, soak the soil in diatomaceous earth, and start all over again.

I share this story because, for me, it is a metaphor for what I think is going to have to happen to truly obtain the healing that's needed within all of our systems and institutions—even the church. There has to be a massive uprooting. Racism and the violence that accompanies it are very much like those squash vine borers. They have infiltrated and attacked our systems. If we're honest, we'll admit that it's an even worse scenario. Our systems were created to provide a home for this "bug." In fact, some would argue that it's not a bug at all but a feature of the system. Nevertheless, even in our attempt to try to Neem oil our way out of the racism that's at the heart of those systems, there's just too much. We've been fighting it for too long. With definite wins along the way, for sure. We've gotten two or three squash of progress out of that work, but we'll be fighting this enemy for much longer with no real guarantee that it won't end up devouring us anyway. Part of our collective reckoning will be figuring out what yanking this thing up by the root looks like. What does a dismantling of the systems that make our country and lives run look like?

I'm not sure the answers are clear yet. Nevertheless, that global work lies mostly at the feet of white folks. The people who for generations have colonized and enslaved and created these systems must be involved in the process of dismantling them. They know where the bodies are. They know where the keys are. They know the secret codes. And yes, there is certainly an intersectional aspect to this. Poor whites will probably have less access to the codes than the "one percent," even if they benefit from their skin privilege. So it will fall on those with intersecting privileges to really begin this uprooting. Whether or not that's possible—whether or not folks are really willing to do the hard, gut-wrenching, soul-transforming work in order to have a better world for our children and our children's children—remains to be seen.

Chapter 8

OH, TO BE SEEN IN THE FULLNESS
OF OUR HUMANITY

*We will heal by exposing our hearts
over and over again.*

Longing to be seen as human, as a people full of creativity and passion and ingenuity, is what makes the physical, psychological, and political violence Black people experience exponentially more painful. Our encounters with racial violence happen early on and are nuanced because in childhood we're often surrounded with people who look like us and who are simply perpetuating the violence they've experienced. While there is this sense that everyone is accountable for their own actions, I think it's important to investigate the power of influences like beauty standards and popular culture.

In elementary school, I was bullied. Part of me is afraid of using the language of bullying, because it has become so normalized. I was mostly taunted because, according to some of my peers, my lips were too big, and my gums were too black. My nose was too big, and my hair was too thick. The ridicule came from both white and Black children, but the most vicious words usually came from other Black kids. It would be easy to say, "Oh well, kids are cruel. This isn't about race," but the nature of the mockery proves otherwise.

The powerful impact of European/white beauty standards has been something that Black and Brown folks have had to manage and reckon with forever. Scholar Susan

Bryant wrote in "The Beauty Ideal: The Effects of European Standards of Beauty on Black Women," "Black women are particularly vulnerable to the effects of European standards of beauty, because these standards emphasize skin colors and hair types that exclude many black women, especially those of darker skin."

Citing the work of M. L. Hunter, she goes on to say,

> Black women today are subjected to incessant messages about European ideals of beauty through family, peers, partners, the media, and larger society. If young black women stand in contrast to what society dictates as attractive, they may find it difficult to grow to accept themselves. As a result, the internalization of racialized beauty standards can perpetuate into a lifelong, intergenerational culture of self-hatred.[1]

It's hard for me, even now, to admit that my experiences as a child may have led to some form of self-hatred. At minimum, I know that I spent many years trying to attain a look that was simply not accessible to me. It wasn't until I was in my mid-twenties that I slowly began to embrace all the things that phenotypically made me Black. The way my skin glows in the sun. The size and shape of my wide, pug nose. The fullness of my lips. The thickness and curves of my frame. The texture of my hair. I've worked to undo the damage and, in the process of talking to other Black women, realized that I was not alone in the mockery I experienced as a little Black girl—even from schoolmates of our own race.

I spoke to a popular blogger and Chicago-based urban farmer, Natasha Nicholes, about the racial bullying she endured as a child:

Grade school is probably where I experienced the most . . . in my life. From a Black dude named Leonard who gave me the nickname "Lips" as a projection and the boys in my class, specifically one who would hurl things like "Pink Ass Baboon" and make noises they considered to be ape sounds whenever I walked by. Eighth grade also found me with random drawings and cut-outs of apes, chimps, and gorillas whenever I came to take my seat. As an apology, I was voted "Best sense of humor," "Most likely to succeed," and "Most athletic." Fun times.

[While] there were lots of things I could get embarrassed about and I did think for a moment I did want smaller lips, I don't think I ever wanted to not be the Black girl I was. I just wanted to be the Black girl who was respected. But that group of clowns weren't worth attempting to get respect from.

[I will say that] nowadays, my skin is thicker, and I'm less trusting of people I am forced to work with because I have no idea when I'll be the butt of the joke. I'm also very quick to speak out for the underdog whenever I hear anyone—child or adult—making off-color jokes. I know that space, and I know how much it hurt to be there.

I'm in therapy to deal with a *lot* of stuff I didn't let roll off my back so easily as a kid, and that's helping. Seeing my kids live unapologetically and also giving them the tools to support themselves when they encounter this type of behavior also feels good.

Natasha's story resonates with my own, so much so that I think it's important to unpack *why* these Black children had decided that the features on my face that were

most African and frankly most like their own were the thing
that should be scorned. Why did these Black children
believe that those particular traits in me were the thing that
they could hurt me with, the thing that they could wield
against me to hurt me?

Because they too had internalized the racial violence
they'd seen. Whether it was the absence of faces that looked
like ours on television or watching the adults in their lives
be on the receiving end of white people's derision, they/we
lived and breathed in a culture that said that what they saw
in me, Natasha, and others had no value. The European
aesthetic of beauty that is given to us very early on says that
a smaller nose or lighter skin or straighter hair is deemed
more beautiful. Naturally, then, if you're an adolescent
coming of age and striving to figure out what's going on
with your body, you are going to gravitate toward whatever
the prevailing standards are in your world. I spent more
time than I care to admit wondering what it meant to be
beautiful. Based on the magazines I read, the music videos
I watched, and the stories told by the people I love, I clearly
knew it wasn't me.

Imagine this narrative in the background as my
seventh-grade crush, the coolest kid in our middle school,
says this awful thing about my lips. I only had eyes for him,
despite not even knowing if he noticed me. But there I
am, on the school bus, caught in the crossfire of two boys
playing the dozens. Suddenly, between the "your mama"
jokes, this same boy whom I'd held up as some kind of well
into which I would willingly pour all my Black tween love
said, "Who would ever want to kiss somebody with lips
that big?"

Of course, in hindsight, my lips were no bigger than
his. But I was devastated. My heart broke into a million

pieces as I replayed over and over again what he said about me. The bus finally made it to my stop, and I got off the bus with tears waiting to burst from my eyes as soon as my feet hit the sidewalk. I cried all the way home.

I told my mom what happened, and while I think she understood on a very surface level that this was a painful kind of bullying, I'm not sure she thought it was a moment that would shift everything I believed about myself going forward. Like Natasha's parents, she gave me the standard advice: "Don't pay him any attention. Nothing's wrong with your lips." For me, however, it was a deep cut in my soul. From that one experience, I stopped smiling fully. By high school, I'd crafted a way of holding my lips that I thought made my lips and gums look smaller. If one looks at any pictures taken of me from middle school until I was about twenty-eight, you will not likely find a single picture where I'm smiling authentically. His words changed everything for me for a very long time.

I suppose I could spend some time reconciling the awfulness of tween boys, but I think we have to target why these particular insults are an extension of the racial violence brandished by white supremacy. Of course, we know that people—especially children, who have no grasp on emotional regulation—often take their own insecurities and project them onto others in order to deal with or manage what they may feel about themselves. But by this logic, these bullies were spewing what they too had been taught about themselves. My seventh-grade crush had learned from somewhere that lips that looked like his, like his mother's, were bad. That violence gave birth to the violence that he, in turn, wielded against me.

These are what I call the little violences, the word "little" being a misnomer because while deemed as insignificant in the larger context, these acts and events still leave an indelible mark. They are often so embedded in our systems, so nuanced, that they become simply a part of our way of moving through the world, yet they are also not something we can shrug off. Little violences attach themselves to our hearts, usually in childhood, and it generally isn't until we are willing to do the work of healing that we figure out they exist and try to unravel from them. Think of little violences like the insidiousness of European beauty standards that affect the way young Black children see themselves, as a way that white supremacy grooms Black and Brown folks for all kinds of more substantial physical and psychological violence down the road. Black women, having heard or internalized our entire lives how we are less than white women physically and intellectually, often find ourselves in adulthood having to navigate work relationships with those same white women. We are forced to decide just how much of ourselves we are willing to give, or better phrased, have taken, in order to survive or thrive in these environments without risk. In this way, Natasha's and my story morphs into Ann's.

Ann Oliver, a sixty-something Black woman in Philadelphia, shared with me her experience on the job:

> After having served as an administrative assistant to an associate director in an institution of higher education within the enrollment management division, a reorganization of leadership had me reporting for eight months to the communications director, who was new to the supervisory role. The associate director was an African American woman, my senior in age by only one year. Although she had a typical extrovert leadership style, I had the ability to

match her assertiveness with my undercover ambi-
vert, which allowed us to be able to simultaneously
respect and embrace each other's roles as supervisor and sistahfriend. With the reorganization, I
reported to a White woman, almost two generations
younger with a democratic style, albeit she may
have had more at stake, and something to prove in
her new capacity. I did not mind; we had interacted
previously on work projects. I was there to continue doing the "exceeds expectations" job I had
done since my first full-time position at the age of
seventeen.

A week before my evaluation was due, we met. I
was stunned to hear her say that she [thought] the
tone of my voice on the phone was sometimes perceived as intimidating and that others agreed with that
assessment, even complained to her. My first thought
was that instead of waiting until the evaluation was
due, the protocol was to have had a midpoint conversation and a timeline for "improving" my customer
service interaction. I sat listening, without comment,
without conveying any emotions, knowing that I
would have the opportunity to write a self-evaluation
on the formal document to be placed in my file. My
second thought was that I was being accused of being
an undercover Angry Black Woman.

On the evaluation form in the employee comments section, I called her out, addressing her
actions as cultural insensitivity as well as lacking in
professional courtesy. And then I signed the document that would go in my personnel file. Now, close
to retirement after forty years of working, the summer
of 2015 will go down as the first and only time in my

employment history that the words "meets expectations" would appear on my evaluation.

Those close to me understood exactly what I did
and why, knowing that I have always believed in the
power of the pen. The few who were concerned,
feared potential backlash, even as they applauded my
response.

That experience remains a reminder of how tir-
ing it must have been for my ancestors to have dealt
with covert and overt microaggressions for which
today's language around diversity, equity, and inclusion is dominant in the wake of George Floyd, Breonna Taylor, and too many others to name. I vacillate
between feeling mentally and emotionally weary, yet
spiritually emboldened, which makes me proud to be
my parents' daughter.

What continues to help me in my healing journey
is [being] an example for others. To not be afraid,
and to pause to allow myself time to think of how I
am to proceed.

There is no doubt in my mind that little violences beget
psychological violence (like the tone policing and power
plays Ann Oliver experienced), which can, if unchecked,
beget physical violence. The entire process is cyclical.
But one of the biggest challenges that Black and Brown
people face today is the way racial violence is portrayed in
the media. We live in a point of time in history where so
much of our lives is guided by the consumption of information via media. There is now a whole a generation who
have never lived without social media or twenty-four-hour
news access. In light of this, so much of what we understand about ourselves and other people is framed by media
portrayals. The negative framing of Black folks and the

often neutral stances on the violence perpetrated against us is another one of those little violences, although I wonder how little it really is, in light of the pervasiveness of the media.

Even attempts to share the news of injustice can unintentionally fall prey to racist framing. Benign images of Dylann Roof, the white-supremacist gunman who opened fire on nine worshipers in Mother Emanuel A.M.E. Church in Charleston, being captured while armed and served Burger King before being jailed contrast sharply with the mugshots or carefully selected (for the prevailing stereotypical narrative) personal photos of Black men and women who'd done way less if any crime at all. Sure, call out the disparity in the way law enforcement are treating these people but also pay close attention to the way these stories show up on our screens. In addition, even victims of police violence cannot escape these negative portrayals. For instance, several years ago, there was an uproar about the pictures of Mike Brown that were selected by the news. It mirrored the way the officer who killed Brown described the child in his testimony—as some demon. The media ran unchallenged with this animalist portrayal until Brown's graduation pic popped up on social media and the imagery was forced to shift.

Adultification is another way the media is responsible for wrongfully framing Black people when it comes to racial violence. Tamir Rice was only twelve years old when he was shot by police for playing in the park with a toy gun. In much of the initial reports, language like "the young man" was used to describe this child. The Cleveland Police Patrolmen Association president said, "Tamir Rice is in the wrong. He's menacing. He's 5-feet-7, 191 pounds. He wasn't that little kid you're seeing in pictures. He's a 12-year-old in an adult body."

The ACLU in Ohio explained the long history of adultification after the officer who killed Rice was not indicted for his murder:

> The fixation on the size of black bodies dates back to America's days of slave auctions, where size was exploited for value and profit. Adultification and attempts to justify physical attacks against black children in America is not new either. In fact, being young did not protect Black children from being lynched in America. From the late 1800s to 1950s Black boys and girls as young as 8 years of age were hanged to their deaths from trees. One such child was 14 year old Emmett Till, killed in 1955.
>
> Today state violence against Black children is expressed through disproportionate school suspensions, arrests, charges, adjudications, bind-overs to adult prisons, and deadly force at the hands of police for similar behaviors as their white peers.[2]

The news media, taking its cues from law enforcement, are absolutely complicit in this kind of framing to the extent that racial violence often becomes the responsibility and even the problem of the victim and not necessarily of those who are perpetuating the crimes.

Something happens to Black people because of the constant presence of the stereotypical narrative. We move through the world with this anticipation of the way we are going to be perceived. It's hard not to expect the negative because it's so damn predictable. The violence we experience at the proverbial hands of the media is the train that's never late. And so we carry the prospect of fear with us. It's not paranoia. We've lived too long with the reality of it. On the rare moments I've chosen to be vulnerable with white people about my apprehensions about a particular scenario or environment, I inevitably get looks of confusion. *Why are you scared? I don't understand the problem.* And the truth of the matter is, they don't understand. (Remember the limits of empathy?) They don't have to live in this Black body.

My intention is to avoid use of the phrase "Black body" as a way to take away the fullness of Black humanity—our spirits, our minds; we are whole people. Yet there is absolutely something about living in this Black body of mine that is significant and unique, and is an experience that someone who doesn't live in one can never understand. Hypervigilance settled into my bones generations before they were even formed in my mother's womb.

Certain thoughts go through my mind that I'm fairly certain don't go through the mind of the average white person. We recently moved into a neighborhood that is relatively diverse but still predominantly white. As a result, I am extremely conscious about my daughter playing in the front yard. Her favorite tree, a weeping willow, is in the front yard, and she likes to sit under it and sing. I know that every time I call her in or tell her to play in the back, I'm stealing some of her wonder, her joy. Yet I cannot help myself. I find myself more concerned about what her Black girl body represents to our neighbors. Even though we have neighbors who are of color, I still feel some kind of way, not about how her spirit or her mind will be perceived, but her body. Her life. I'm acutely aware that any negative perception a neighbor may have has likely been framed by media— news channels, digital media, and Hollywood—and would not likely align with whom I know her to be.

The conversation around representation and why it matters has, on one side, a respectability component, right?

We want certain images of Black folks to be in the forefront because we want to be seen in a particular light. I know that if my white neighbors can regularly see positive reflections of Black people who are well-rounded, complex human beings on both the big and small screen, then maybe they won't judge my child harshly for singing a bit too loud or doing one too many cartwheels. Maybe they will lose their assumptions because they've been exposed to these characters that somehow resemble the ones who live in their neighborhood.

The problem with this line of thinking points to the whole empathy question again. Can white people truly see Black people enough to engage them as they would anyone else? Black celebrities and high-profile people often have their Blackness erased by some white people and therefore are still not seen in the same light as the Black family down the street. Their fame somehow relieves them of their identity. There are numerous accounts from Black celebrities who experience racist encounters with white people when the latter do not realize who they are. Once their celebrity is discovered, there is a shift. Some white folks have gone as far as to say, "Oh, you are not *that* kind of Black person." This would be a fascinating study in the way the brain categorizes people based on exposure—if it weren't also incredibly violent. We know that it only takes one time for a white woman to not recognize someone as "that kind of Black person" for that person to potentially end up dead. And since most Black people are not famous nor do we have high profiles, it still means that our value as humans is much lower to white people who don't *see* us.

None of this changes the fact that we need a diversity of roles and images in the media. Black folks in real life aren't always thugs or prostitutes or slaves or the sassy sidekick. And even if we were, thugs, prostitutes, and sassy sidekicks are worthy of love and care too. We are also not always the wealthy, against-all-odds members of the Talented Tenth—Black folks we've seen in recent years on television.[3] And even if we are, the wealthy Talented Tenth are worthy of love and care too. In fact, those of us in the middle and who are most likely to live down the street or around the corner from the average white person have just as much right to our humanity, to the assumption of goodness and the receipt of lovingkindness—the literal "love your neighbor as yourself" treatment. We are fully human beings filled with the good, bad, and ugly just like everyone else.

But the experience of racial violence born from racism is so much more than just a distraction perpetuated by the media. As much as I believe in the power of rest and stillness and turning off the noise, it's still way too easy to say, "Turn off your screens" or "Ignore Hollywood" or "Don't buy that product" without considering how the proliferation of these media narratives impacts a Black person's immediate world. Racial violence can disrupt a person's mental, emotional, and spiritual state, leading to cases of PTSD and complex PTSD. The way this violence is positioned in the media does the same.

In 2004-ish, I had just broken up—for the last time—with someone I'd been dating off and on for a good while. I knew it was the end because in all the previous breakups, I was emotionally rocked. Lots of tears. A constant back-and-forth about who was right or wrong. He wielded his verbal abuse like a machete, chopping my soul each time.

You'll never meet someone who will deal with you.
Who in the world is going to love you?

By the time I'd arrived at that final conversation, I'd heard enough. I knew I needed to make sure that this was a completely clean break and that I never returned to this relationship with someone who made me feel like I was indebted to him, that I wasn't good enough. I'd had enough of feeling inadequate in my past. I didn't need to be with someone who affirmed my negative self-talk.

So this time around, the breakup was less emotionally tumultuous. I was still devastated, but I could access peace. I basically told this person in our last conversation, "God bless you," and hung up the phone. I was done.

My response afterward was not as good. Instead of seeing the relationship as information, a way to know what I did or did not want, I closed my heart off to love. I actually had enormous capacity to love. But after being in a verbally and emotionally abusive relationship, I had come to a point and time in my life where loving felt risky.

I didn't want to feel small anymore. That's what I thought love meant because that's all I'd experienced and all I'd observed. With every subsequent date, I'd meet people, enjoy their companionship, but my heart was hard. I didn't know I could set boundaries, hold standards, and also allow myself to be gentle. Softening felt like weakness, and that weakness felt like I would be left exposed to hurt and harm and danger in a way that I just wasn't willing to do. It didn't matter that I may have met someone who had no intentions of hurting and harming me. I anticipated it.

About a year later, I did meet the man who eventually ended up being my husband. And the truth is, in the beginning, I was extremely hard. At least I tried to be. I was demanding in all the ways I didn't want to be. Again, I needed to feel safe, and this was the only way I knew how to be. The ironic thing? It wasn't as if when he didn't meet my expectations, I was going to leave. He'd exhibited a good amount of what I wanted. I just wanted to feel in control.

What I learned in the three years I dated my husband before we got married was that exposure is part of love. Opening yourself up to something new, even to the potential of being harmed, was part of the journey—because there was also the greater potential of being connected to a love that is greater than anything you can imagine. It may look different than you thought, but that's okay.

Here's the catch: Being willing to open yourself up to love despite past pain and hurt actually gives you *more* capacity to love. You actually gain the ability to hold more love, the more you love. But when you shut yourself off, when you decide that this person or this thing is not worth giving your heart to, then the pain wins. You don't have the capacity to nurture or curate any more love in your life. And guess what? In the context of race and racism, this lesson is the hardest but most necessary.

As believers, we are called to love. But on many days, the risk of loving white people is not worth it. My past and supremely valid lived experience says that loving them the way God wants me to opens me up to the potential for violence. But I also understand that when I don't allow myself the opportunity to experience love and joy with whomever is sent in my path, I am limiting myself from the expansiveness of love available to me. And frankly, some days—just like all those years after the breakup—I'm okay with that. Sometimes we need time to heal before jumping back into the fire.

To be clear though, this cuts both ways.

Some white people might feel like they can avoid being confronted with their own biases or racism by not engaging with Black people at all. It's a perverse kind of out-of-sight, out-of-mind dance they do. But what they don't realize is that when they engage with content that only supports their narrow worldview and choose to not even try to have healthy relationships with Black people, then they are the ones who are losing. They have limited their own capacity to experience the kind of love and joy our particular culture can bring into their lives—which, though I'm clearly biased, is glorious on its own.

The point of so many well-meaning diversity and inclusion efforts is, yes, to ensure equity. But also, I think, at their core, these efforts must be about amplifying this notion that you, white person, actually benefit by engaging with and getting to know people like me. Our workplace, organization, neighborhood, or church is culturally richer because I'm here.

If we all held the view that we are going to open our hearts and minds to every opportunity for love, joy, and peace God puts in front of us, regardless of our past experience and with reasonable consideration of the potential for harm, then the act of loving itself becomes the gift. It is going to increase our capacity to love those who actually deserve our attention. Loving my neighbor as myself is a gift to the neighbor, sure, but I too gain from it. I get to have more fertile experiences as a human being on this planet.

A transformation can happen if we just figure out how to replace the constant exposure to and experience of violence that Black and Brown folks have. That's where challenging the media's narratives and stories becomes essential. Maintaining awareness for the sake of activism and change while limiting the desensitization that comes with constant exposure is not an easy balancing act. Some days I need to look that trauma and grief in the face. I have to read Cousin Vickie's obituary again to reference it in an article. I have to follow the latest hashtag to get information on how I can help. But for the sake of my mental, emotional, and spiritual health, I can't look all that in the face every day. What would it mean to allow images of Black joy and love to live alongside the evidence of injustice—not to replace the hashtags but to add to them? Because, remember, two things can be true, right? We can hold perpetrators of racial violence accountable while also reveling in the holistic images of Black life. One does not negate the other. They actually serve each other well. This is what it might mean for us to heal—reimagining a world where we can hold this pain because we are also holding joy.

These are the questions: How do we amplify images of love and joy within the Black community, among Black folks, or even between Black and white people? How do we allow those images to live alongside the things that need to be done in order to procure justice and allow people to see that the racial violence and the lived experience of Black folks is true and painful? Is it even possible to hold both of these things simultaneously so that, hopefully, one of those acts of love and joy will overtake those acts of violence?

The biggest challenge with this whole conversation about exposure, love, and representation is actually an issue of spiritual proportions. *All* the physical and psychological violence happening in America right now, including racial violence, is truly an object lesson in the perils of idolatry. The rape and sexual assaults of women and children, the deaths of numerous young unarmed Black men going unprosecuted, the compassionless ranting of alleged conservatives with hiding-in-plain-sight political agendas . . . all of this exists because we have chosen to make idols of men and women. Too many people, including those who profess Christ, have elevated police officers

and celebrities and government officials and political affili-
ations (on both sides of the aisle) above what the Spirit is
showing and prompting us to do and be in this earth. For
example, some people determined that former president
Barack Obama was too Black for the office, while others
claimed he wasn't Black enough. Police officers like Derek
Chauvin have GoFundMe accounts created in their name
where people have raised thousands of dollars for a man
who clearly murdered another on camera—all because of
the blue of his uniform, the bling of his badge, and the color
of his victim's skin—all because of what those symbols mean
to white folks in this country. We have Black celebrities still
bleaching their skin to adhere to beauty standards that say,
as my mother used to quote, "Light is out of sight, Brown
can stick around, and Black get back." As long as we continue to buy into all of this, we are bound to never be able
to rightly discern the truth and stand for what Christ stands
for. We will remain impotent. We will not heal.

Chapter 9

A NEW NARRATIVE

*We will heal through authentic acceptance of the
whole story and embracing our freedom work.*

I have no idea why I chose to do something so ridiculous.
It was one of those things you hear your aunties and uncles
at the annual Black family reunion talking about when
describing the crazy stuff white folks do. But there I was
thinking about participating in the Polar Bear Plunge on
New Year's Day 2018.

My family had decided to take a holiday trip to the
Jersey Shore, about an hour away from our home. Something about the water has always drawn me to it. I find it
extremely healing. So on the first day of every year, I try
to make sure I'm near some body of water—a lake, river,
stream, or creek, it doesn't matter. So that year, we were
staying at a hotel directly on the beach in what is usually
a ghost town that time of year. But in 2018 we started seeing way more people than usual. We weren't sure what was
going on, but honestly, we didn't really care. We were simply enjoying the heated pool, taking some walks on the cold
beach, looking forward to the New Year's Eve fireworks,
laughing, and enjoying our family time.

On New Year's Eve, I happened to see a man at
the pool who was basically immersing himself in the deep
end, over and over again, and doing these weird dives. My
daughter, being the only extrovert in our family, swam over
to the man, arm floaties flailing, and asked the man what

he was up to. He said he was preparing for the Polar Bear Plunge.

The what?

The Polar Bear Plunge is essentially an event that happens every New Year's Day where a bunch of people—yes, mostly white folks—will run into the freezing ice-capped ocean, some diving in head first, and then run back out. Afterward, they wrap themselves up in towels and coats and party the rest of the day.

My first thought? Umm, no. Definitely a white-people thing.

But then something indescribable came over me. I can't attribute it to anything else but the Holy Spirit. I began to see the plunge not as just some extreme white people's challenge but as a ritual, a rite of passage I needed to do. It was at a time of significant transition in my life, and I needed something to symbolize my willingness to accept discomfort and do something completely out of my comfort zone.

"I want to do that."

"Sure you do," my husband said.

I guess my face revealed just how resolute I was because his mouth fell open.

"Are you serious?"

Yes. I was so serious.

The next day, we went out there. We were three brown specks in a sea of white, and most of them looked at us like we were aliens. But I had on my swimsuit and was determined to run out there into the deep and take my leap of faith. And when the horn blew, I threw off my coat, ran twenty feet into the surf, and dived in (although not head first). It was the most terrifying and invigorating thing I've done. It felt like a different kind of baptism. Something had changed in me. My willingness to do something that ten years ago would have had me rolling my eyes was the first sign I'd changed. Enduring that momentary discomfort while holding onto the hope that my life could reflect the symbolism of trusting what I could not see or anticipate was an even more powerful shift for me.

Up until then, I'd had a very shallow approach to many areas of my life, maybe even to how I dealt with racial trauma. There was a fear of going deeper, of unearthing the pain. This would shock people who know me because many already think I'm deep. But diving into that ocean taught me to never settle for my own mediocrity just because it's someone else's best, and resisting going deeper spiritually, physically, emotionally, and relationship is mediocre at best for me. The polar plunge was a demonstration of being willing to uproot some stuff and be uncomfortable in order to heal.

The ocean has always been a metaphor in my life. It's beautiful and majestic and yields only to the heavens. It's also fearsome and vast and filled with dangers seen and unseen. You can wade in it safely on the shore or take the risk and dive into its depths. But in all its power, the ocean restores. It revitalizes. I had to be willing—against all elements and around those who clearly didn't get me and likely didn't know why I was there—to take the leap. Dive in. I had to strip down and run toward something I knew was better, regardless of my fears or who was with me. No matter if it was on record. Why? Because there was a little girl watching who was seeing her mama do things that other mamas she knew didn't do—and that would teach her to stand true in her own identity and do what she is led to do with abandon and without apology.

In previous chapters, I've talked about the personal steps we all must be willing to take to heal from racial trauma and violence. To be clear, there is absolutely a link between the individual and the collective. For Black and Brown people, as a collective, healing requires reckoning with the impact of trauma, embracing grief, and pursuing wholeness. For white Christians, healing requires an untangling from their ancestral mandate of colonization and false notions of supremacy.

Another part of the collective healing will come when white people, in the aggregate, are willing to be fully account-able for the pain that has already been inflicted. Maybe it feels like I've been saying that over and over again—like playing a broken record—because I have. Nobody wants to feel like they're personally responsible for the devasta-tion of whole groups of people, but having a more collective mindset will help white people realize the necessity of tak-ing ownership of the traumas that the creation of whiteness has wielded. This hopefully will lead to white people mak-ing room for all the ways in which Black folks show up—in anger, sorrow, or joy; in the fullness of our humanity—as opposed to just the ways that make them comfortable.

I've spent the last few years writing about what I call "Black joy." It's the idea that Black and Brown folks experience a particular kind of joy as a result of having to be resilient. It's the result of staring in the face the oppres-sion we experience and deciding to live anyway. We tap into the joy that already exists in us as human beings and, if we must, weaponize it against those who try to dehumanize us. Black joy shows up in a number of different forms, so it's certainly not monolithic. But when we're talking about racial violence, our healing will require us to shift the nar-rative from solely being about the generational traumas that

Black folks experience, and the ways in which racial violence devastates us in our communities, to also speaking aloud the generational joy we retain despite it all. Black joy is that intangible thing that keeps us going and fighting and trying to heal even if we don't do it right all the time. Black joy helps us rip the pain from our experiences out at the root and plant new seeds.

As much as I am desperate to center the stories of Black people as a way of demonstrating our resilience, I also want to challenge white folks to do what is absolutely necessary, the uncomfortable thing, to take the deep dive, to unravel themselves from that ancestral legacy in order to be able to see a future that is much more aligned with the love, peace, and joy that the Christ we follow intended.

My humanity keeps me hopeful that there are white people out there who really get it, ones who really have the kind of empathy needed to do the hard work of dismantling white supremacy at the root. Yet if I'm honest, sometimes the joy killer has been learning that even those who call themselves allies are not able to fully release all that comes with whiteness in order to make room for how God might use Black folks. I see this evidenced in the unwillingness to submit to Black leadership whether within the church or outside of it. There is still sometimes a resistance to sitting with the lived experience of Black people without saying, "Oh, you're making such a big deal out of this," or "Maybe it wasn't that bad," or "I'm sorry that that happened to you, but that's not everyone," or, yes, "All lives matter."

A colonizer energy allows for even allegedly progressive white Christians to co-opt the discourse in order to make themselves appear like they are doing good, godly work. In reality their actions are more what I like to call "ally adjacent," meaning that if it doesn't require that much sacrifice, then of course they'll black out their social-media profile picture or show up at a protest. In a 2020 Twitter thread, activist Brittany Packnett Cunningham further defined the current roles and stances of white people in movements for social justice. She wrote, "ALLIES care but act when convenient. Allies take little risk to their comfort & seek personal recognition for momentary action. ACCOMPLICES take on more risks & more often get in the way of oppression. They disrupt, but engagement may vary with privilege. CO-CONSPIRATORS know they are not free until everyone is free & act like it. They don't just disrupt, they build. Not episodic actions, but ever-evolving mindsets and lifestyles. They seek permission from the most oppressed & listen more than they speak."[1]

I'm reminded of the passage in 2 Samuel 24 when David, preparing to give an offering to God, says, "I will not offer burnt offerings to the LORD my God that cost me nothing" (v. 24). It would be heartening to see white Christians apply this same lens to their offerings in social justice movements and their engagements with Black people in general. The truth is, if your allyship is not costing you anything, is it really love you're demonstrating? In fact, maybe that kind of sacrificial love, to which we are all called, should be at the center of the way white people show up when racial violence is enacted against Black folks. Doing so doesn't just make more room for our trauma; it also makes room for our joy.

Whenever I'm asked about how I am healing from my experiences with racial trauma in general, and specifically my cousin's murder, my answer changes from day to day. Sometimes I feel like I'm on the other side of my grief journey and there is light. Other days, I feel like I'm being smacked around by those same cold waves I dived into ten months before she was killed. Other days, I just don't know. It's a nebulous reality I've had to accept. The biggest trap that the enemy of our souls has set, especially for believers, is this false notion of certainty. I've written so much about this, but I truly believe that much of our need to be certain is deeply connected to our traumatic experiences.

Let's think about what happens to the body when we experience a traumatic event that's not processed normally. Neural pathways are formed that send our brains information every time we even remotely encounter a similar circumstance. In turn, our body seeks safety at every turn. Whether via the responses of fight, flight, freeze, or fawn, we start to rely on things, beliefs, theologies, or ideologies that make us think there's a possibility of safety. We double down on these beliefs—lean into the certainty—in an effort to ground ourselves in something that feels steady. Part of my personal healing journey has been to release it all, to accept that certain things aren't certain at all.

In a very tangible way, healing for me has looked like intense therapy. I've spent the last several years talking to a therapist, almost weekly, about grief and the journey to accepting uncertainty, fear, and more. It's taken a long time to even be able to talk about the grief, not to mention do the work around healing from it. I've done everything from breathwork to grounding exercises to meditation in order to give myself grace and space to heal. I'm also incredibly grateful for my study of Christian contemplation, which holds so many keys to managing trauma. In many ways, it is the opposite of what I grew up learning about Jesus and God.

What I love about Christian contemplation is its emphasis on stillness. Being open to the movement of God through silence has taught me how much *being* is an important part of my identity. I'm acutely aware that much of my identity is deeply connected to who I am as a Black woman, a writer, an artist, but I'm learning that my life is equally valuable without any of that. I can *be*, and God is pleased. Studying the philosophers in the contemplative tradition has helped me release performance as a measure of my worth. The psychological violence that comes with racism and white supremacy taught me that I needed to do that dance. I needed to be conscious and concerned about the white gaze. And even when the great Toni Morrison told me that there would be a "little white man that sits on your shoulder and checks out everything you do or say, [but] you sort of knock him off and you're free,"[2] I still found it hard to do until I became still enough to hear the voice of God reflected in my own inner voice. Then I grew increasingly comfortable with my Blackity-Black self, with no window dressing or contortions, and despite any violence acted against me.

All my life, I'd performed for my worth. I did what researcher and writer Brené Brown calls hustling for my worthiness. So, if anything, therapy and contemplation have helped me release my need for control. Morgan Harper Nichols, an artist whose powerful words and images of affirmation have been popularized on social media, once wrote, "Of course, you can't control outcomes and there is no way to predict what other people will do in their lives, but it is possible to be loving without being controlling. To be hopeful without toxic positivity. To dream without ignoring reality."[3] I accept the fact that literally nothing I can do can stop a white person from seeing my brown skin and deciding I should die because of it. It's terribly possible that I could be the next hashtag. And as deeply devastating as that reality is, it's also a liberating feeling to know that because I can't do anything about it—because I'm not in control—I don't have to do a dance to try to prevent it from happening. As a matter of fact, I'm inherently worthy.

I know this stands in conflict with the theology of original sin, but one thing I know for sure is that, from the inside out, I've been worthy of living free since the day I was born. Are there times when I slip back into a mode of thinking that causes me to worry about what white folks are going to say or think? Sure. Even writing this book was an exercise in regularly kicking that little white man off my shoulder. But at the end of the day, my healing journey, my liberation, and the liberation of my people is so deeply tied to an understanding that I am and we are inherently worthy. No societal definition driven by whiteness or white supremacy can ever fully account for who I am; for who we are. Writer and activist Prentis Hemphill said it best: "Healing is the work of getting other people's stories out of your system: other people's shame out of your body."[4]

As I'm constantly considering the ways in which we can heal from the kinds of racial violence Black people have experienced and some white people have either wielded or been complicit in allowing to continue, I can't help but think about my first hiking trip. A friend of mine invited me to come along with a hiking group she was a part of, and on another whim, another girlfriend and I jumped in the car and drove two hours to Bear Mountain in Upstate New York. It was definitely something outside of my comfort zone because I'd never hiked for real. I had a lot of misperceptions of what the experience would look like. *What about bugs? Or animals? What if I get halfway to the top and I can't make it any farther?* I definitely felt fearful anticipation in my body. Climbing to the top of that mountain was both something I wanted to accomplish and something I was scared to accomplish.

When we started the hike, the lessons started hitting me right out of the gate. We were walking along a paved road for about fifteen minutes, and I was pleasantly surprised. *Oh, this is cool. The gradient isn't that steep, and the road is paved. No big deal.* I had done those kinds of walks through state parks, so it was familiar—at least until our guide told us to turn left so that we could begin the *actual* hike. When I looked to my left, there were rocks and trees and the literal side of the mountain.

"Wait, where's the path?"

"Oh no, we are going to climb up," she said with a grin. "There's definitely a path there, but we are going to have to climb over some rocks and move some brush out of the way. This is what it means to hike through the woods."

I'm not too sure about this.

The lesson was clear, though. There's not always an easy road to where you're trying to go. The road may start off smooth, but it will likely turn rocky because you are elevating. I see that in my own healing process. I initially thought it was just going to be about getting a massage every now and then or going to therapy. But then there was a point in time when things went left and even in my therapy I had to do more intense work. My grief began to show up in all kinds of ways—tears, anger, frustration—and so modalities like eye movement desensitization and reprocessing (EMDR) helped me become clear enough so that I *could* pray or meditate. My therapist helped me understand that going through the hard place, digging through life's proverbial brush, is part of getting to where you need to be. You're moving up. You're getting closer. But the healing isn't at the top of the mountain; it's in the process of walking up it. I think for Black folks, the key to beginning to heal from racial violence is understanding that sometimes people won't get what we're doing. Some things are going to come up that feel really hurtful and really painful. We deserve the smooth paths sometimes, for sure. But dealing with other humans can also mean climbing those rocks. But we're still in the climb, right?

For white folks, it's a bit different. It's also about not turning away from the hard places or looking for the easy route, but it's about sitting in the discomfort too: accepting the horror of what your ancestors have done, even what you might have done, to marginalized groups and allowing that pain to reveal what's missing in you.

Another lesson of that hike was the importance of frequent rest. After I'd finally embraced the fact that we were actually climbing this mountain, I became frustrated because it felt like we'd walk five minutes, then stop. The guide would say, "Take a drink, sit on a rock if you need to, and then we'll continue on." Then we'd climb/walk another five minutes, then stop again. This wasn't the way I operated. I was the kind of person who preferred to push through until we were done. There was no time for stopping. *Let's hurry up and get there*, and I said as much to the guide.

The guide helped me with this too. "To be a good hiker and make it to the top, you must take frequent moments to breathe, hydrate, and rest. Otherwise, you'll run out of energy and not be able to continue. The refueling is what keeps you going."

Oh, so the thing that feels like a hindrance, like it's slowing you down, is actually the very thing that's giving you the stamina you need to reach your destination. We can actually go higher and further if we take the time to breathe and rest frequently along the way. So yes, for Black folks, there is so much change that still needs to happen, so much work to be done. Even in social justice circles, the work has a constant push and pull. There are marches to organize, people to galvanize, and policies to change. But even as we're pushing through to get these things done, we must take frequent moments of rest. We must stop and breathe if we want to actually see our work come to some kind of fruition.

Probably the most amazing lesson from the hike came from the most unexpected place. It was right before spring when we went, so there wasn't much in the way of greenery yet. When we got to a certain height on the mountain, we could look back at how far we'd come, which is a lesson all by itself. But when we looked back, we saw all kinds of trees with no leaves. Everything looked dead. Everything looked as if it would never live again. But in reality, those trees were simply waiting for the season that would best allow them to flourish—and although we couldn't see it, they were still being nourished underground.

Black, white, Latinx, Asian, or Indigenous: there will absolutely be times when you look back at how far you've come on your healing journey and everything looks like scorched earth. Especially when you are fighting for your life and/or the lives of marginalized people, you might look back and see that you've moved further along, but you may also see the stuff that you thought died along the way. It's important to realize that some of that stuff isn't dead. It's just being nourished in a place where we can't see the fruit yet. It's just waiting for its season. For me, the process of healing from the violence I've experienced often sends me to a place of just wanting it to be finished. I've said so many times to my therapist, "Can this just be done? Can I just not feel these things anymore? Can I just be healed already? I'm not sure if these grounding techniques or this meditation is working because I'm still struggling. I'm still being triggered."

But what I miss in those moments is that something is happening in my heart during this process. I can't see it yet. But my spirit is being fed what it needs so that when the right season comes, it can reveal the evidence of my healing. But I have to focus on doing my work. Even while hiking, my guide would keep telling me to keep my head up and stay focused on my own steps. I'd started to worry about how far up someone else was or how far behind I was, but the guide was adamant: "No, just focus on what's in front of you. Look at the ground, look at your feet. Yes, pay attention to what's around you, but also focus on the mark." I was thinking I needed to actually see the markers to know where we are, and she hit me with, "That's why you have a guide, so you can focus on your path and enjoy the journey. Allow me to guide you."

Ultimately, beyond whatever theologies we embrace, the Holy Spirit is our guide—not to mention the legions of ancestors, that great cloud of witnesses cheering us on and interceding on our behalf. If we call ourselves people of faith and followers of Jesus, then we know we have a guide, so we can trust that and follow our path. We can keep our eyes focused and enjoy that journey, knowing that we are being guided in the direction of our healing.

Remember all those dead trees? Well, they weren't all bare and brittle. In our final leg up the mountain, I was shocked to see a fully green tree growing out of the side of the mountain. I saw a pile of rocks and stones and in the middle of one rock was bark connected to bright green leaves: a literal tree growing out of the stone. I couldn't help but let the tears flow at that point. It was like a message that said good stuff can grow out of hard places.

Sometimes you have to climb high enough to see those kinds of miracles. We have to trust that when we're on this healing journey, when we're trying to reconcile the kinds of racial violence Black folks have experienced over multiple generations, that reckoning is hard. The path is rocky and bare. But if we continue to fight for our healing, we might get high enough to see the miracles. We might get to see a tree growing out of rock. We might actually see a change in policy or a change in this country that we never could have anticipated and never would have expected because we hadn't arrived at that point yet.

I often wonder if this country wants to heal, or if the wounds are too deep and the pain too great to ever come back from our history. I wonder if grace can ever really be a thing here—not because God is not sovereign and powerful but because we have long walked away from the power available to us through grace. So many of us complain—with legitimate reason—about how racism and racial violence have permeated every aspect of our culture and the systems that drive it, but I wonder if we really want to know the source of our issues enough to make lasting and sustaining change. Clearly, implementing laws and legislating equity, though necessary, doesn't fully change how people feel about each other. It doesn't change how or if we engage one another with compassion, whether we can truly see each other as *imago Dei*. So there has to be something else, right? A willingness to unearth all the trauma to heal. We need to call a thing a thing and tell the whole story so that we give it air and it no longer has the power to seep into our bones and ignite the synapses in our brains that have already been rewired to accept white supremacy and hatred as the norm. Dismantling our systems at the root seems like the only way to right the wrongs, and that's scary. The disruption of the status quo for white folks feels like the biggest challenge to shifting the culture of violence.

What keeps my hope alive is that I'm constantly reminded that good things can still grow out of hard places. Sure, they're nurtured differently. And maybe they're hard to see. But I encourage us all to do our work. Yes, the healing work for white folks is different and maybe much more extensive than for Black people. But it's the only way we'll be able to see those trees growing out of rocks, those miracles we never could have imagined.

Healing is always about liberation. It's always about freedom. And it's about a personal freedom that doesn't impede on another people's liberation. For too long, the narrative has been that in order for whiteness to feel free, to have liberty, there needed to be a marginalization of everyone else. That was the basis of colonization, enslavement, and inequality. It was believed that in order to succeed, to thrive, to cultivate, there *had* to be a degradation, a diminishment, a violent dehumanization of those who do not look like those in power.

That's not healing. Global healing from the trauma of racial violence is about finding a way to facilitate liberation and freedom for everyone that doesn't impede on anyone. That is the challenge. Healing can't happen alongside a belief that the freedom of Black and Brown people somehow makes white folks less free. A complete, self-actualized, God-ordained healing at both the individual and collective levels is about pursuing liberation. Jesus came so that we might be free of any who would hold us back from whom God created us to be. Yes, the demand for liberation may require revolution. It certainly will require a major upheaval of thought and action—a willingness to open ourselves up to a kind of love that challenges us and everything we've known.

It's challenging to talk about healing and freedom with a very real and looming presence and potential for physical and psychological violence. I readily admit that sometimes love and joy as weapons don't feel like enough. But I think it's because my perspective is earthbound. My ancestors would see it differently. My ancestors who fought with actual weapons, who shed blood in this liberation work, knew that the only way they would be able to survive that bloodshed was through protecting and maintaining their humanity through the power of love and joy. This is ultimately what I wish for us all.

NOTES

INTRODUCTION

1. Martin Niemöller, "First They Came," as cited at https://www.hmd.org.uk/resource/first-they-came-by-pastor-martin-niemoller/.
2. David F. Krugler, *1919, The Year of Racial Violence: How African Americans Fought Back* (New York: Cambridge University Press, 2015), 3.
3. Michelle Alexander, *The New Jim Crow: Mass Incarceration in the Age of Colorblindness* (New York: New Press, 2010), 24–25.
4. Michael E. Ruane, "A Brief History of the Enduring Phony Science That Perpetuates White Supremacy," *Washington Post*, April 30, 2019.
5. Niemöller, "First They Came."
6. James Baldwin, "An Open Letter to My Sister, Angela Davis, by James Baldwin," in Angela Yvonne Davis, *If They Come in the Morning: Voices of Resistance* (New York: Third Press, 1971).

CHAPTER 1: WHY BLACK TRAUMA MATTERS

1. Vanessa Caitlynn Facemire, "Understanding the Insidious Trauma of Racism: An Exploration of the Impact of Racial

Socialization, Gender, and Type of Racist Experiences," PhD dissertation, University of Akron, 2018, http://rave.ohiolink .edu/etdc/view?acc_num=akron1525285448114384.

2. Lisa Firestone, "The Trauma of Racism," *Psychology Today*, June 4, 2020, https://www.psychologytoday.com/us/blog /compassion-matters/202006/the-trauma-racism.

3. Joy DeGruy, *Post Traumatic Slave Syndrome: America's Legacy of Enduring Injury and Healing* (Portland, OR: Uptone Press, 2005), https://melaninandhoneydotcom.files.wordpress .com/2016/07/degruy-joy-post-traumatic-slave-syndrome.pdf.

4. Alicia St. Andrews, "Post Traumatic Slave Syndrome and the Invisible Wounds of Trauma," San Francisco County ACEs Connection, March 9, 2016, https://www.pacesconnection .com/g/san-francisco-county-ca-aces-connection/blog/post -traumatic-slave-syndrome-and-the-invisible-wounds-of-trauma.

5. James Baldwin, "Letter from a Region in My Mind," *New Yorker*, November 17, 1962, https://www.newyorker.com /magazine/1962/11/17/letter-from-a-region-in-my-mind.

6. Rochaun Meadows-Fernandez, "The Little Understood Mental-Health Effects of Racial Trauma," The Cut, *New York*, June 23, 2017, https://www.thecut.com/2017/06/the-little -understood-mental-health-effects-of-racial-trauma.html.

7. Venita Blackburn, "White People Must Save Themselves from Whiteness," *Paris Review*, March 25, 2019, https://www .theparisreview.org/blog/2019/03/25/white-people-must-save -themselves-from-whiteness/.

8. Kenneth V. Hardy, "Healing the Hidden Wounds of Racial Trauma," *Reclaiming Children and Youth* 22, no. 1 (Spring 2013): 24–28, https://static1.squarespace.com/static /545cdfcce4b0a64725b9f65a/t/54da3451e4b0ac9bd1d1cd30 /1423586385564/Healing.pdf.

9. Christopher D. DeSante, "Working Twice as Hard to Get Half as Far: Race, Work Ethic, and America's Deserving Poor," *American Journal of Political Science* 57, no. 2 (April 2013): 342–56, http://www.jstor.org/stable/23496601.

10. Bessel A. van der Kolk, *The Body Keeps the Score: Brain, Mind, and Body in the Healing of Trauma* (New York: Penguin, 2014), 98.

CHAPTER 2: IT'S ALL INTERSECTIONAL

1. "Kimberlé Crenshaw on Intersectionality More than Two Decades Later," *Columbia Law News*, June 8, 2017, https://www.law.columbia.edu/news/archive/kimberle-crenshaw-intersectionality-more-two-decades-later#:~:text =Crenshaw%3A%20Intersectionality%20is%20a%20lens ,class%20or%20LBGTQ%20problem%20there.

2. LaShawn Harris, "#SayHerName: Black Women, State-Sanctioned Violence and Resistance," *The American Historian*, https://www.oah.org/tah/issues/2020/history-for-black-lives /sayhername-black-women-state-sanctioned-violence-resistance/ (accessed February 24, 2022).

3. Michelle S. Jacobs, "The Violent State: Black Women's Invisible Struggle against Police Violence," *William and Mary Journal of Race, Gender, and Social Justice* 24, no. 1 (*William & Mary Journal of Women and the Law: 2017 Special Issue: Enhancing Women's Effect on Law Enforcement in the Age of Police and Protest*) (2017): 39–100.

4. Marisa Iati, Jennifer Jenkins, and Sommer Brugal, "Nearly 250 Women Have Been Fatally Shot by Police since 2015," *Washington Post*, September 4, 2020, https://www.washingtonpost .com/graphics/2020/investigations/police-shootings-women/.

5. Danté Stewart, "If people in the Hebrew Bible can imagine God as a sun and shield, then black people can imagine God as black and, as Alice Walker writes, the Ultimate Ancestor," Twitter, October 6, 2021, 9:49 a.m., https://twitter.com /stewartdantec/status/1445748016799903744?s=20&t =iTUNo5ctwg_DQP5ST_oraA.

6. Chimamanda Ngozi Adichie, "The Danger of a Single

Story," TED Global, July 2009, https://www.ted.com/talks
/chimamanda_ngozi_adichie_the_danger_of_a_single_story
?language=en.

CHAPTER 3: JUSTIFIED BY LAW

1. Felice León, "How American Slavery Helped Create
Modern-Day Policing," The Root, August 20, 2019, https://www
.theroot.com/how-american-slavery-helped-create-modern-day
-policing-1837411350.

2. In León, "How American Slavery Helped Create Modern-
Day Policing."

3. Sonya Ramsey, "The Troubled History of American
Education after the Brown Decision," *The American Historian*,
https://www.oah.org/tah/issues/2017/february/the-troubled
-history-of-american-education-after-the-brown-decision/
(accessed February 24, 2022).

4. Kidada E. Williams, *They Left Great Marks on Me: African
American Testimonies of Racial Violence from Emancipation to
World War I* (New York: NYU Press, 2012), 4–5.

5. Imani Perry, "She Changed Black Literature Forever.
Then She Disappeared," *New York Times*, September 17, 2021.

CHAPTER 4: SILENCE IS VIOLENCE

1. Toni Morrison, "Nobel Lecture," The Nobel Prize,
December 7, 1993, https://www.nobelprize.org/prizes/literature
/1993/morrison/lecture/.

2. Alexus Rhone, email message to author, 2013.

CHAPTER 5: "WHAT ABOUT CHICAGO?"

1. Jameelah Nasheed, "'Black-on-Black Crime' Is a Dangerous Myth," *Teen Vogue*, July 28, 2020, https://www.teenvogue.com/story/black-on-black-crime-myth.
2. Walter Brueggemann, *The Prophetic Imagination: 40th Anniversary Edition* (Minneapolis: Fortress Press, 2018).
3. *The Negro Motorist Green Book* was a travel guide for Black people during the segregation area that offered a list of safe towns and cities as well as motels and restaurants for those who did not want to encounter racial violence while traveling.

CHAPTER 6: FADING EMPATHY

1. Resmaa Menakem, *My Grandmother's Hands* (Las Vegas: Central Recovery Press, 2017), 5.
2. Popularized by western evangelicals, the "Romans Road to Salvation" is a way of explaining the path to salvation to an unbeliever using select verses from the book of Romans in the New Testament.
3. Martin Luther King Jr., "The Other America," speech at Grosse Pointe High School, Grosse Point, Michigan, March 14, 1968, https://www.gphistorical.org/mlk/mlkspeech/.
4. *James Baldwin: The Price of the Ticket*, dir. Karen Thorsen, *American Masters*, Public Broadcasting Service, August 14, 1989.

CHAPTER 7: THE REAL CAUSES OF WHITE VIOLENCE

1. Zora Neale Hurston, "How It Feels to Be Colored Me," *World Tomorrow 11* (May 1928): 215–16.

CHAPTER 8: OH, TO BE SEEN IN THE FULLNESS
OF OUR HUMANITY

1. Susan L. Bryant, "The Beauty Ideal: The Effects of European Standards of Beauty on Black Women," *Columbia Social Work Review* 11, no. 1 (July 11, 2019): 80–91, https://doi.org /10.7916/cswr.v11i1.1933.

2. "Black Children Are Children: Tamir Rice and the Adultification of Black Bodies," ACLU of Ohio, January 8, 2016, https://www.acluohio.org/en/news/black-children-are-children -tamir-rice-and-adultification-black-bodies.

3. Out of concern for the overemphasis of Black people choosing agricultural routes to success, a concept developed in 1903 by sociologist W. E. B. Dubois suggests that there should be an emphasis and necessity in higher education on educating the most able 10 percent of African Americans.

CHAPTER 9: A NEW NARRATIVE

1. Brittany Packnett Cunningham, https://twitter.com /mspackyetti/status/1265320049050636292.

2. *Toni Morrison: The Pieces I Am* , dir. Timothy Greenfield-Sanders, Perfect Day Films, 2019.

3. Morgan Harper Nichols, "You're Allowed to Imagine Something Better," *Storyteller*, September 21, 2021, https://www .thestorytellerco.com/blog/youre-allowed-to-imagine-something -better.

4. "Eyes on the Prize: Hallowed Ground," produced by Prentis Hemphill, HBO Max, August 19, 2021, https://www .hbomax.com/feature/urn:hbo:feature:GYQ1PRAGVlcLCJwE AAAA9.